Unit 29

*Prepared by Cicely Havely for the Course Team
in consultation with Jennifer Drake-Brockman*

Water Pageant for Queen Elizabeth (1591) at Elvetham, Hampshire. The pool is crescent-moon-shaped in Elizabeth's honour, and contains a Ship Isle, a Snail Mount, a Castle and an island Cavaliero (raised battery position).

INTRODUCTION

This week we are going to look at another renaissance: in Elizabethan poetry. Like the Italian Renaissance in art, much of its inspiration came, if not from a rediscovery of classical forms (they had not all been lost) at least from a fresh look at them. The Middle Ages had valued classical literature for its didactic and moral content. The men of the Renaissance looked for a beauty of more than doctrine.

The Elizabethan Renaissance came late, and after two false starts. Chaucer (1340?–1400) had been in touch with the Continental literature of his time, and was acknowledged by his heirs to be a master of European stature. But no one had matched him. In the early part of the sixteenth century Sir Thomas Wyatt and the Earl of Surrey had tried to reintroduce Continental manners and refinements into English poetry, but both men were dead by 1547, and no one followed them.

In this unit we shall look at how the Elizabethan poets saw themselves. First, we shall look at their attitude towards the classics, and their doubts about their own ability ever to do as well. Second, we shall look briefly at their response to the greatest modern poetry – the Italian. Third, we shall look at what they thought of, and learned from, Chaucer. Fourth, we shall look in detail at a representative group of poems to see how some of the Elizabethans approached the challenge of classical and European standards. Finally, we shall make a minor 'case study' of Edmund Spenser, the poet most admired by his contemporaries because he had achieved what they all wanted for their literature. We shall be concerned this week more with theory and style than with typical themes – some of which you will be studying next week. My aim in this part is to help you make a historical effort, and see the Elizabethans not just from the viewpoint of the 1970s.

Before you begin work, it would be useful to spend an hour or so working through your set text: The Penguin Book of Elizabethan Verse, *edited by Edward Lucie-Smith. Read whatever catches your eye. In that way, if this subject is completely new to you, you will at least be able to begin with an impression, however faint, of the quality of Elizabethan poetry.*

1.0   THE ENGLISH LANGUAGE AND ELIZABETHAN WRITERS AND CRITICS

We'll begin about sixty years before our period: in this extract from a longish poem written in about 1504, the author complains about the inadequacy of his native tongue.

> Our natural tong is rude,
> And hard to be ennewed
> With polysshed termes lusty;
> Our language is so rusty
> So cankered and so full
> Of frowards,[1] and so dull,
> That if I wold apply
> To write ornately
> I wot not where to find
> Terms to serve my mynd.

[1]perversities

John Skelton: *The Boke of Phylyp Sparowe.*

6

Arts: A Second Level Course

Renaissance and Reformation   Units 29–30

Elizabethan Poetry

Unit 29 prepared by Cicely Havely in consultation with Jennifer Drake-Brockman

Unit 30 prepared by Brian Stone

The Open University Press

Cover illustration: Memorial portrait of Sir Edward Unton, c. 1596 (National Portrait Gallery)

The Open University Press
Walton Hall Bletchley Bucks

First published 1972

Designed by the Media Development Group of the Open University.

Printed in Great Britain by
EYRE AND SPOTTISWOODE LIMITED
AT GROSVENOR PRESS PORTSMOUTH

SBN 335 00663 9

This text forms part of the correspondence element of an Open University Second Level Course. The complete list of units in the course is given at the end of this text.

For general availability of supporting material referred to in this text, please write to the Director of Marketing, The Open University, Walton Hall, Bletchley, Bucks.

Further information on Open University courses may be obtained from the Admissions Office, The Open University, P.O. Box 48, Bletchley, Bucks.

CONTENTS

General Introduction to Units 29–30

Cicely Havely wishes to acknowledge helpful criticism from Brian Stone and Prudence Smith in the preparation of Unit 29.

Brian Stone wishes to acknowledge material supplied by Catherine King and John Ferguson in the preparation of Unit 30, and helpful criticism from them and from Cicely Havely, Colin Russell, John Purkis and Francis Clark.

Although these two units were written separately, the study scheme for Elizabethan Poetry which they contain was conceived as a unity. We suggest that first of all you read the short introductions to the two units (Unit 29, first three paragraphs; Unit 30, Section I) before reading the rest of this general introduction.

The set text for these two weeks is *The Penguin Book of Elizabethan Verse*, ed. Edward Lucie-Smith, 1965. All the poems which we ask you to study are either in this book, or in the text of this correspondence material, or in the additional poems printed at the end. The latter are all numbered, and are referred to in the text by their numbers.

The single recommended critical reading support text is the Oxford Paperback *Elizabethan Poetry, Modern Essays in Criticism*, ed. J. Paul Alpers, 1968 Oxford University Press, 1967.

The gramophone record accompanying Units 29–30 was prepared by Brian Stone and produced in the BBC studios by Helen Rapp. On the first side, there are poems and extracts from poems set for study, spoken by Gary Watson. On the second side, in the preparation of which Philip Olleson was music adviser, are lute-songs, the words of which either figure already in the set book, or are included in the additional poems. The singer is John Elwes, and the lutanist Timothy Davies.

The broadcasts associated with these two units are:

Television: 'Gloriana'	— presented by Cicely Havely
Radio: (1) 'Popular Poetry in the Elizabethan Period: The Traditional Ballads'	— presented by Ewan McColl
(2) 'Popular Poetry in the Elizabethan Period: The Broadside Ballads'	— presented by Ewan McColl

The radio programme for Unit 31, 'Satire in Shakespeare's Time' presented by Brian Stone, relates more to the poetry than to the drama.

The broadcasting supplement for Elizabethan England, Units 28–34, gives study details and other guidance connected with these broadcasts.

Was the English language itself good enough for poetry to rival the classics? This was what worried poets of the early sixteenth century. English had long been considered adequate for mere entertainment – story-telling and the lighter kinds of moral debate – and of course it was used for everyday household communication. As you will see in the *Introduction to English Renaissance Drama* (Week 31) the vernacular was also used for moral teaching of the unlearned in miracle plays and sermons. But did it possess the qualities necessary for the creation of work fit to stand with that of Homer and Vergil? That was the question.

Note: In some, but not all, of the quotations in this unit, I have retained the original spelling.

1.1   The Italians had had to fight the same battle for their language. Dante wrote his treatise on the possibility of an Italian poetry, *De Vulgari Eloquentia*, in Latin, but he wrote his greatest work in Italian, following the same patriotic urge that impelled later English writers (and French and German and Spanish and Dutch) to write in their own languages.

There was no standard form of English at the beginning of the sixteenth century. If you wrote in Latin all your readers would be on an equal footing. But regional dialects were then almost like different languages, and people of different areas wrote as they spoke. The vernacular didn't just vary from place to place; it changed in time too. Chaucer's English was clearly different from that of the sixteenth century. Again, Latin had the virtues of solidity and permanence. Before the vernacular established itself completely it seemed to some writers that there was a serious incongruity in trying to cast lasting truths in any but an unchanging language.

1.2   Consider the following extract from *The Elementarie* (1582), a work on the education of middle-class children, by Richard Mulcaster (1530?–1611), who was Spenser's headmaster, and a champion of the English language. Then answer in your notebook the three questions which follow it.

> There be two speciall considerations, which kepe the *Latin* and other learned tungs, tho' cheflie the *Latin* in great countenance among us, the one thereof is the knowledge which is registered in them, the other is the conference which the learned of *Europe* do commonlie use by them, both in speaking and writing . . . Is it not in dede a mervellous bondage, to becom servants to one thing for learning sake, the most of our time, with losse of most time, whereas we maie have the verie same treasur in our own tung, with the gain of most time? Our own bearing the ioyful title of our libertie and fredom, the *Latin* tung remembering us, of our thraldom and bondage? I love *Rome*, but London better, I favour *Italie*, but England more, I love the *Latin*, but I worship the *English*.

1   What are the two advantages of Latin?
2   What is the chief *practical* advantage of replacing it with English?
3   What is the chief *emotional* advantage?

Did you find that passage quite difficult to understand?

Discussion of Mulcaster

1   (i)   The wisdom of the past has been recorded in Latin ('the knowledge which is registered . . .'). Mulcaster implies that Latin is the language of learning.
    (ii) It is an international language ('conference').

2   It would save time!

3   Mulcaster is proud of his country and his language and thinks it an indignity ('thraldom and bondage') not to use his own language for learned matters. Remember that Rome and Latin meant not just the city of antiquity and its language, but the Pope's city and the language of the Roman Catholic Church. There may well be an anti-Popish sentiment here.

1.3   One of the most eminent critics of the English language was *Roger Ascham* (1515–68), Latin Secretary to Queen Mary, and Tutor to Queen Elizabeth. I suppose he might be said to have had a professional interest in maintaining the superiority of Latin over English. However, he rather grudgingly agreed to write his treatise on archery, called *Toxophilus* (1545) in English in order to benefit 'the gentlemen and yeomen of England', but he devotes much of the *Preface* to the praise of the classical languages:

> As for ye Latin or greke tongue, every thyng is so excellently done in them, that none can do better: In the Englysh tonge contrary, every thyng in a maner so meanly, bothe for the matter and handelynge, that no man can do worse. For therein the least learned for the moste parte, have ben always mooste redye to wryte. And they whiche had leaste hope in Latin, have bene moste boulde in englysche: when surelye every man that is moste ready to taulke, is not moost able to wryte.

1   What does Ascham mean by 'matter and handelynge'?

2   Try to estimate why he thinks 'matter' should be worse in English.

Did you find Ascham easier to understand than Mulcaster? Who was writing earlier? (Don't write, just check and decide.)

I'm sorry to be able only to give you a short piece of Ascham, because to my mind he writes beautifully. Look how carefully the sentences are divided and balanced. It is ironic that someone who thought English an inferior language should in fact have been of considerable influence in the development of a simple English prose style.

Ascham's prose is far more 'polysshed' (the word used by Skelton and others) than Mulcaster's: yet it was written almost forty years earlier. This is a practical example of one of the things that the pro-Latinists complained about: the lack of fixed standards in the vernacular. Mulcaster, an educationalist, finds it difficult to express himself simply and directly in his native language on a problem which most of his schoolboys could have put into lucid and unambiguous (if unexciting) Latin.

Discussion of Ascham

1   Content, or substance; and style, or presentation.

2   He implies that the time and mental energy it takes to translate one's first (English) thoughts into Latin will be repaid with an increased value in the sentiments and beauty in the style. To write what one has to say in Latin is good precisely because it stops you writing as you think. He is suggesting that if the use of Latin is encouraged, only the most learned and most worth-listening-to will write.

1.4   However, I think Ascham conceded his own defeat here. Like every author he wanted the widest possible audience, and so he wrote *Toxophilus* in English. The reading public was, increasingly, not the same as the Latin reading public. The invention of printing meant that books were already getting cheaper, and a new generation of readers was growing up who were not scholarly enough to want to read Latin. Indeed, Latin was receiving official discouragement. We have already seen in Mulcaster a possible example of antagonism towards the traditional language of the Church. But this, of course, began much earlier. English Bibles were placed in the Churches from about 1538 onwards.

A reading from the Bible in English and an English Litany (probably by Cranmer) had been introduced into English Church services in 1544, the year before publication of Ascham's book. Four years later there was an English form of the Communion Service; English prayer books were issued in 1549 and 1552 – the latter being the original of the revised Prayer Book familiar today. The first *authorized* English Bible was 'Mathew's Bible', largely the work of William Tyndale, who said that he wanted to bring it about that a ploughboy (who would not of course know any Latin) would know more of the Scriptures than learned bishops. Opponents of the Bible in English said it was casting pearls before swine, but their reactionary views were overwhelmed by the widespread urge to educate those ignorant of the learned languages in matters both spiritual and secular. Other objections were that the English Bible contained heresies (which cannot detain us here) and, as you might have expected, that the English language simply was not good enough to express the word of God. But such objectors were fighting against the tide. Once English was officially considered good enough for the Bible, and for use in the services of the Church, the argument that it was not good enough for matters of high importance quickly began to fade. Thus the triumph of the vernacular is closely bound up with the Reformation in England.

Although English gradually became acceptable, it was still acknowledged that it needed improvement. Our business this week is what Ascham called 'handelyng'. What sort of attempts did the Elizabethan poets make to improve the beauty of their language? We shall at first be largely concerned with translation from the classics – an obvious way of trying to bring into the English language the respectable qualities of the ancient tongues.

1.5　First, look at a very extreme example: *Richard Stanyhurst's* translation of *Vergil* (set text, p. 263). You may think it's dreadful stuff. You may quite like its eccentricity. Make a list of those features of the language which seem to you *un-English*.

When you have done that, read Barnabe Barnes's *Sestina* (p. 38), another very extreme example. Whatever you think of it, the technique certainly commands some admiration, even if your ultimate reaction has to be, Why bother? See if you can work out how he arranges his rhyme scheme.

Discussion of Stanyhurst and Barnes

I don't propose to give you an exhaustive list of all Stanyhurst's linguistic eccentricities, but here are some of the more obvious ones, which you should have noticed:

Compound words: the English language will tolerate simple compounds like hard-froze; and hair-locks and hail-knob don't sound too un-English. But Stanyhurst drastically extends the range of compound forms in a way which doesn't sound right at all: May-fresh, huntspears, gold-stood, Lucifer-heav'nly-In-beauty, bedmatch, over-ambling.

Word order: often abnormal – see the last line, for example.

Odd-sounding verbal participles: becrampound, bepowdered.

Archaisms and rusticisms: yoonckers, hoblobs, gambols, hopping, hogsters, jumble.

Excessive alliteration and assonance: for example, prinking not pranked with trinkery trinkets; rumbelo thund'ring rattleth.

Stanyhurst is trying to aspire to the virtues of Greek and Latin by bending his English into their patterns. Take his word order for example: he often uses inversions of what is normal in English. Greek and Latin are inflected languages – that is to say, the parts of speech show what their function in a sentence is by a variable word ending – and so they can be arranged in any order, and still be understood. When Stanyhurst arranges English words in a Latin order, we have to work harder to deduce the likely sense. Similarly, verbal adjectives are a more prominent feature of Latin than they are of English. Compound words are particularly common in Greek heroic poetry, and so Stanyhurst tries to make English enlarge its frontiers there. And even those rustic words like 'yoonckers' and 'hoblobs' which look as if they might be good native stock without a trace of Mediterranean influence on them – well, their inclusion is after the most venerable classical precepts: when Theocritus, a Greek poet of the third century B.C., wrote the pastoral poems that Vergil and nearly every subsequent poet of any pretensions imitated, he fitted his 'handelyng' to his 'matter', and put into the mouths of his shepherds old-fashioned and rustic words of the Doric dialect that suited their occupation and their remote dwelling-places. If you look again at Stanyhurst you will find that *on the whole* rustic words are attached to rustic people. (The qualification is necessary because Stanyhurst, as you've probably guessed, is often more enthusiastic than discerning.) Whatever the quality of his execution, the principle is important: choosing a style to fit your subject was called *keeping decorum.* We shall meet it again.

Far from trying to expand the frontiers of his language, Barnes at first sight seems to be fencing himself in with insurmountable problems. But he too is testing his language; seeing what sort of performance it puts up under stress. The restrictions he put on himself suggest he was aiming at elegance and refinement. In my estimation he achieves nothing but a curiosity. Yet Edward Lucie-Smith mentions his 'strange obsessional effects'. Is that what you find there?

The rhyme scheme of the sestina, which was fixed by the inventor of the sestina form, Arnaut Daniel, a knight troubadour from Perigord who was in the entourage of Richard Coeur de Lion, is certainly complex to the point of obsession, but not, I think, very effective. The six lines of each stanza always end with the same six words, the sixth becoming the first of the next stanza. The pattern begins again in the seventh stanza. If you've analysed further details of this pattern, well done! I find it more complicated than beautiful.

1.6   Of course, most attempts to refine and improve the language were less extreme. Dandyism of language was despised, as you will see from this extract from a work you have met before, Sir Thomas Elyot's *The Boke Named the Gouernour* (1531) (ed. S. H. Croft, London, 1883):

> Who that hath nothing but langage only may be no more praised than a popinjay,[1] a pye,[2] or a stare,[3] whan they speke featly.[4] There be many now a dayes in famouse scholes and universities whiche be so moche gyven to the studies of tonges onely, that, whan they write epistles, they seme up the reader that, like to a trumpet, they make a soune without any purpose, where unto men do herken more for the noyse than for any delectation that ther by is meued. Wherefore they be moche abused that suppose eloquence to be only in wordes or coulours of Rhetorike, for, as Tulli saith, What is so furiouse or mad a thinge as a vaine soune of wordes of the best sort and most ornate, contayning neither connynge nor sentence?

[1]parrot [2]magpie
[3]starling [4]well

Elyot is talking about empty rhetoric. (He is talking about the malpractice of schools and universities, and so may mean humanist Latin style as well as English.) Rhetoric is the art of deploying words not only skilfully (so that they communicate an author's sense) but also persuasively (so that they can please or disgust us at the author's will). I suppose we tend to think of a poet relying on his ear and his instincts to create pleasing effects, but a Renaissance poet thought of himself as a craftsman who had to learn his trade under a rigid discipline. The middle English word for a poet, 'maker' embodies this notion, and although by the late sixteenth century it was considered hopelessly old-fashioned in Southern England (a good example of the regional variations in the language I mentioned earlier) Sir Philip Sidney used it in his *Apolgie for Poetrie* (*c.* 1580). As Sidney pointed out, the word 'poet' itself comes from the Greek verb *poiein*, 'to make'. Barnabe Barnes probably thought of the stiff test he set himself as an exercise in rhetorical dexterity: once he has mastered such an exceedingly difficult task he would be able to set about simpler things with a more practised grace. But for us, his poem has more style than sense. To use Ascham's words, it is all 'handelynge' and no 'matter'.

One of the tasks a Renaissance poet would set himself in his apprenticeship would be the diligent study of the classics. But even among those who could read Greek and Latin most found it a laborious and time-consuming business – a fact which (you should remember) Mulcaster regretted, and Ascham applauded. Translation was the obvious answer. It would communicate the revered matter or content of the ancient writers at the same time as providing modern poets with an opportunity to prove that their expression or 'handelynge' was no way inferior.

> To be skilfull and exercised in authors translated, is no lesse to be called learning, then in the very same in the Latin or Greeke tunge . . . the translation of Latin or Greeke authors, doeth not onely not hinder learning, but it furthereth it, yea, it is learning it self, and a great staye to youth, and the noble end to whiche they oughte to applie their wittes, that with diligence and studye have attained a perfect understanding to open a gap for others to folow their steppes, and a vertuous exercise for the unlatined to come by learning, and to fille their minde with the morall vertues, and their body with civyll condicions, that they maye bothe talke freely in all company, live uprightly though there were no lawes, and be in a readinesse against all kinde of worldlye chaunces that happen, whiche is the profite that commeth of Philosophy.
>
> Sir Thomas Hoby, translator of *The Courtyer*
> by Baldassare Castiglione, ed. W. E. Henley, 1900.

I hope you noticed that Hoby is plugging the moral benefits of being able to read the classics in translation. Elizabethan society contained both a residuum of the medieval doctrine that learning was only good if it enhanced virtue, and the beginnings of the Puritan suspicion of pleasure for its own sake. (More of this in Unit 31.) And so they constantly claimed that literature should both please and instruct.

1.7   We have forgotten how to read long poems. Chapman's Homer, Golding's Ovid, and Marlowe's translations and imitations are not much read by students now, and Elizabethan poets are admired chiefly for their short lyric poems. But I want you to see something a bit more like the whole picture, and so I want us now to read some extracts from long poems which are also translations, partly to see if they really deserve total neglect.

First, read the extract from Chapman's translation of the *Odyssey* (p. 70). It was this translation, you may remember, that for Keats was like the discovery of a new world:

> Then felt I like some watcher of the skies
> When a new planet swims into his ken . . .

I'm struck by an alien quality in the verse too. Of course, a part of the poem which is about the world of the dead is likely to be untypical. Even so, not a word seems to concede a jot to his own civilization. (Compare Stanyhurst's translation of Vergil's 'pronuba' as 'Chaplain'.) The idea of a blood-sacrifice which the dead must taste before they can communicate with the living must be abhorrent to a Christian reader, yet Chapman permits neither disgust nor approbation to modify his tone, which is throughout austerely pagan.

Unlike most Elizabethans, Chapman set out to be an exact translator of both meaning and mood. He wanted to make his English reproduce the qualities of the Greek, yet he was enormously proud of the innate qualities of his own language, as this extract shows:

> If Italian, French and Spanish have . . . not . . . thought it any presumption to turne him into their languages, but a fit and honourable labour and (in respect of their countries profit and their poesies credit) almost necessarie, what curious, proud and poore shamefastnesse should let an English muse to traduce him, when the language she works withal is more comfortable, fluent and expressive; which I would . . . prove against all our whippers of their owne complement in their countries dialect.
>
> George Chapman, *A Defense of Homer*,
> Elizabethan Critical Essays Vol II,
> ed. Gregory Smith, Oxford University
> Press, 1904.

You can see from this that the production of good poetry was a matter of national prestige.

Chapman's methods of making English emulate Greek are not Stanyhurst's. His choice of words is simple and unaffected and his word order is seldom different from that of normal English prose. Yet there is some experimentation here too. Chapman also found it necessary to create new words: underline some of them.

Look at the lines 'There clustered then . . . sorrows were' (l. 7 ff). The choice of words is subdued and thoughtful: 'much suffering' is an austere phrase, to my mind deadened by those repeated 'u's' and the similar 'ch' and 'ff' sounds; it was not selected for its beauty alone, but for its sense. 'Soft' and 'tender' are not striking or unusual epithets, but then, death is common – 'timeless': they convey pity, rather than agony. 'Timeless' is a slightly difficult word; it asks for a pause of thought. It makes eternity mean not time without end, but no time; the world of the dead is a place where time does not exist. Notice how the pieces which make up the sentence are varied in length, so that the mounting pace of the sentence is stately and sonorous. But it does not end dramatically, at a climax; it fades with a sweet sad word: 'and *green* their sorrows were'. This fading of the verse is in complete accord with the subdued, forlorn wistfulness of the wraiths, whose sadness is not loud. The choice of words is perfectly poised against their sense. For me, Chapman is a master of one of the most admired principles of rhetoric. I have referred to it already. Can you remember what it was called?

Now I want you to look in the same way at another part of the same extract: the lines 'I know that, sailed from hence . . . the dear societies'. Write in your notebook a brief account of Chapman's choice and deployment of his words.

DISCUSSION

Chapman doesn't so much create new words, as try to extend the meanings and usage of the old ones: *bereft* normally requires 'of'; *unmeasured* means here 'endless' or 'numberless'; *Exciteful* has a meaning that would normally be carried in a verb: here it is adjectival – prayers to arouse, or excite the gods. In my judgement, none of Chapman's usages are difficult to understand, but they help to give his language that strange, alien quality I talked about earlier. As for the account of part of Elpenor's speech that I asked you to write, well, I'm not going to discuss it. Read again what I wrote earlier, the passage, and what you wrote: I think you will know whether you have given an adequate rendering of Chapman's tone and expression. The practice of fitting words to sense is called '*keeping decorum*'. I shall discuss it more fully later (Section 3.2).

1.8   Now read Arthur Golding's translation of *Ovid's Metamorphoses: Medea casts a spell to make Aeson young again* (p. 129).

Unlike Chapman, Golding is not concerned to make an accurate translation, so much as an *English poem* out of Ovid. His world here is still supernatural, but it has some touches that bring it nearer home: 'witchcraft', 'wizards', 'elves' are words from a forbidden world, but the same English world of magic and superstition as *A Midsummer Night's Dream*. Words like 'welkin' and 'whist' emphasize the deliberate 'Englishing' of Golding – the former an already archaic word meaning 'sky', frequently used by poets who wished to glorify the richness of their native past. It is no wonder that Golding's translation has been referred to as 'Ovid in English dress'.

You have already come across the tradition of 'moralizing Ovid' (Units 5–6). Do you think that Golding still wants to moralize – or is he more interested in communicating the beauty and the magic which the passage holds for him? If your answer to the first part of this question is 'Yes', where is your evidence? (Make a mark in the text.) If 'No', what changed climate of opinion does this indicate?

Discussion of Golding

I can find no trace of a moral purpose in this extract – he does not condemn Medea for her black arts, but makes you feel her beauty. It would be wrong to think that morality in art was no longer considered important (look at Hoby again) – but Golding's translation is an indication that attitudes were more relaxed. Renaissance writers were no longer quite so embarrassed by the pagan beliefs of writers they enjoyed. They valued pure beauty in art more highly, and were content that the didactic element should be less obtrusive.

1.9   Now turn to the extract from *Christopher Marlowe's* translation of Ovid's *Amores* (p. 182) and write in your notebooks a brief description of your response to this piece and the next – the passage from *Hero and Leander* (p. 183) – which is not a translation, but an imitation of classical models.

If you didn't know which piece of Marlowe was a translation, you might imagine that the first piece was his own, because there the classical references are less integral, more purely figurative and decorative. So translation merges naturally into the whole body of Elizabethan poetry.

Discussion of Marlowe

It is, I think, easier to judge Marlowe's achievement in the translation than the imitation. Self-confidence, sensuality and worldliness come over unmistakably in the first, made harmonious by a vivid perception of beauty – 'such light as twinkles in a wood'. But in the second Marlowe seems less sure of himself. I find the lines

> There might you see the gods in sundry shapes,
> Committing heady riots, incest, rapes

rather comic – and I'm not sure whether they were meant to be. Perhaps Marlowe was still glad of Ovid to lean on.

1.10   Before we move on to look at translations from modern languages, I want us to consider one further short-lived influence Latin and Greek had over English: *quantitative verse*. Perhaps you noticed that Stanyhurst's rhythm is, by our standards, completely irregular.

Now, you may have thought that scansion was simply one more thing that Stanyhurst wasn't very good at. But read *Sir Philip Sidney*'s poem *Oh sweet woods, the delight of solitariness* (p. 240).

Sidney is not a careless writer. Look how grave and deliberate is the construction of the second verse. And yet, once again, the same awkwardness of rhythm. Mark in where you think the light and heavy stresses fall in the first four lines of the second stanza. You will see that if we judge by stress patterns, which normally regulate English verse, then this is irregular.

Twice could be a coincidence, so read the *Phaleuciacs* by the unknown writer A.W. (p. 34). Once again you will notice that the rhythm does not seem to fall naturally.

Discussion of Sidney

But if instead of marking stress, we mark long and short syllables, then a regular pattern emerges.

$$- \quad - \quad - \quad \cup \quad \cup \ - \quad - \quad \cup\cup - \cup \quad -$$
Oh sweet woods, the delight of solitariness!
$$- \quad - \quad - \quad \cup \quad \cup \ - \quad - \quad \cup\cup - \cup \quad -$$
Oh, how much I do like your solitariness!
$$- \quad - \quad - \quad \cup \quad \cup \ - \quad - \quad \cup \ \cup \ - \quad \cup \quad -$$
Here nor treason is hid, veiled in innocence;
$$- \quad - \quad - \quad \cup \quad \cup \quad - \quad - \quad \cup\cup \ - \quad \cup \quad -$$
Nor envy's snaky eye finds any harbour here . . .

What Stanyhurst, Sidney and A.W. are doing is to imitate classical metre. It's a complicated subject, and I don't want to do more than reinforce the points I've made already: that English poets wanted to write poetry as good as their classical masters, and that their attempts led them into various kinds of serious experiment. The use of this rhythm is based on principle, not on crankiness.

Very briefly: our familiar metres are based on stress or accent, but in Latin and Greek poetry, the metrical arrangement of words depends not on accent, but on the length of a syllable. Classical metres have a regular number of syllables to the line arranged in patterns according to their length. Try to say Sidney's poem aloud.

This is the metre of Horace's first Ode. I think you'll agree that the decision about whether a syllable is long or short has in some cases been very arbitrary. A.W.'s choice is the metre of one of Sophocles' choruses. It is not easy to follow, and I suspect that metre, rather than sense, influenced his choice of words.

1.11   I hope you will agree that the most successful of the pieces in classical metres which you have read is Sidney's, though even that falls unnaturally on the ear. Why should poets carry their emulation of Latin and Greek authors to this extreme point? The debate lasted over forty years from the time of Roger Ascham (whose reluctance to use English at all we have already seen) to *Thomas Campion*, who claimed in 1602, when the failure of many experiments should have told him how wrong he was, that Latin metres sounded perfectly natural in English. Two of his examples are in your anthology: the *Anacreontic verses* (p. 62) and *The eleventh epigram* (p. 63). Campion claims that they prove his point, but what do you think?

1.12   Samuel Daniel replied to him in an essay full of shining good sense: he dares to assert that the classical authors were not altogether perfect.

> Every language hath her proper number or measure fitted to use and delight, which Custome, intertaininge by the allowance of the Eare, doth . . . make naturall . . . The striving to shew their changable measures in the varietie of their Odes, have beene very painefull no doubt unto them [the Latin poets] and forced them thus to disturbe the quiet streame of their wordes, which by a naturall succession desire to follow in their due course. But such affliction doth labour – some curiositie still lay upon our best delights (which ever must be made strange and variable), as if Art were ordained to afflict Nature, and that we could not goe but in fetters . . . Me thinkes we should not so soone yeeled our consents captive to the authoritie of Antiquitie, unless we saw more reason: all our understandings are not to be built by the square of Greece and Italie.
> *A Defence of Rhyme;* Elizabethan Critical Essays, ed. Gregory Smith, Oxford University Press, 1904.

The date of this essay is 1603. Daniel's words have the ring of perfect confidence.

2.0   THE ITALIAN INFLUENCE

The poets of the Italian Renaissance were the heirs of Rome and honoured in England almost as much as their ancestors. Poets of the early sixteenth century like Wyatt and Surrey looked to them as proof of what a modern language could achieve, and translated and imitated them to learn their skills in much the same way as they imitated the classics. Later translators from the Italian do not look like apprentice craftsmen: read the extracts from *Harington*'s translation of Ariosto's *Orlando Furioso* (p. 148) (and Harington's other poems as well – I think you'll be amused by them); and from *Fairfax's Godfrey of Bulloigne* – a translation of Tasso's *Gerusalemme Liberata* (p. 118). Of course, these are only brief extracts from very long poems; but I think we can see that both poems are very much at home in English. As translations, you will have to take my word for it that they are tolerably accurate. But even without the Italian, I think you might guess that both authors cared more to make good English poetry than an accurate reflection of their Italian originals.

Indeed, as your editor points out, Fairfax consciously imitated an English poet in his translation! The style, like the subject of both poems, is highly sophisticated – certainly not a mindless copy of just the sense of a foreign language.

2.1   Italian is a very musical language, and its influence on English metre and verse forms is probably its greatest contribution to Elizabethan literature. We have already looked at the abortive attempts of some poets to foist classical quantitative metres on to English poetry. Italian metres were far closer to our own, and since the lyrics of the Middle Ages, English poetry had always exhibited an aptitude for variety in metre and stanzaic form. It would take too long to discuss the range of metres in your anthology, so I shall simply ask you not to ignore them, and ask yourselves in each poem you read, what the form and metre contributes to the whole. Remember too that many of the lyrics were meant to be sung. Ask yourself what difference that would make.

2.2   One form, however, we should single out: the *sonnet*, first used extensively by Petrarch, and introduced into England in the early sixteenth century. The sonnet, properly, has fourteen lines, each of ten syllables, in English. (But be careful: the Elizabethans sometimes called *any* short poem a sonnet.) Apart from this, considerable variation is possible. Often there is a strong break in the thought after the eighth line. The first eight lines are called the octet, and may be divided into two quatrains; the last six lines are the sestet. Or the sonnet may be divided into three quatrains and a final couplet which contains the summing-up or climax, often wittily expressed. This latter is the more common English form of the sonnet.

Read: *Daniel – Let others sing of knights and paladins* (p. 79); *Drayton – How many paltry, foolish, painted things* (p. 105); *Sidney – Having this day* (p. 238); *Spenser – Let not one spark* (p. 251). Write out the rhyme-scheme of each sonnet, calling the first line and all that rhymes with it 'a', the second 'b' and so on. Then comment on the form of sonnet you identify, and try to decide why the sonnet was so popular.

Discussion of the sonnet

Daniel: abab cdcd efef gg; three quatrains, a 'turn' in the sense between each, possibly strongest after the second; the whole summed up in the couplet. Drayton: the same. Sidney: abab abba cdcdee; no break in sense, the couplet the climax. Spenser: ababbcbccdcdee; three interlocking quatrains, no sense-break, the couplet a kind of after-word.

I think it was the combination of flexibility and discipline that made the sonnet so popular; the challenge lay in the need to fit a thought into a form that would then enhance that thought. It's a substantial form too, not long enough to be ponderous, but able to support quite complex thought. Nearly every Elizabethan poet tried his hand at the sonnet and many wrote lengthy 'sequences' of them. We shall be meeting more sonnets later.

Not only the forms, but the style and subjects of Italian poetry were imported into English. In particular, love poetry of this period owes much to Petrarch. Neo-Platonic ideas too, are very pervasive, and as you already know, derive from Italy. I shall not discuss these further aspects of Italian influence here, however. But you will meet them later in this unit, and extensively in Unit 30.

3.0 CHAUCER

Poets at the beginning of Elizabeth's reign felt rather ashamed that there had been no English poet of European stature since Chaucer. He had been a renaissance all on his own. He had travelled in Europe and his works reflect the influence of Dante, Petrarch, Boccaccio and the authors of the French romances. When the English Court still spoke French he wrote poetry that was fashionable then and moving now in English, adopting many French words where his own language was too harsh or inadequate, but espousing the cause of the vernacular as devotedly as Dante had done. All I've been able to include for you to look at is two brief extracts from Chaucer's work, but you will find suggestions for further reading after Additional Poems 2.

3.1 The first extract (Additional Poems 1) is a description of the heroine of the *Knight's Tale* from the *Canterbury Tales*. The story is about the rivalry of the two men who fall in love with her; at this moment both are prisoners. The second (Additional Poems 2) is from *Troilus and Criseyde*: the shy lover Troilus has been taken to Criseyde's bedside by her practical, worldly uncle Pandarus (from whose name we get the word 'pander').

In these extracts you will find two worlds: one is solely of the imagination – beautiful, idealizing and fragile. The other claims to be entirely down-to-earth, bluff and 'realistic'; it is scathing of the delicacy of the other world. Which extract represents which view of the world, and what evidence can you put forward to support your views?

Discussion of Chaucer

Emily's world is idealized, unblemished spring-time and love at first sight; Pandarus's is practical and down-to-earth – he scoffs at Troilus's faint-hearted prayer. Troilus himself, however, is speaking the language of Emily's world. The point of the distinction I have asked you to make here will be apparent later on.

3.2 Now I want us to look at Chaucer's reputation amongst later poets and critics.

Read the following Elizabethan opinions of Chaucer, and answer my questions:

> *Gascoigne:* our Mayster and Father.
> *Sidney:* After whom Chaucer and Gower encouraged and delighted with theyr excellent foregoing, others haue followed, to beautifie our mother tongue . . . I know not whether to mervaile more, either that he in that mistie time could see so clearly, or that wee in this clear age walke so stumblingly after him. Yet had he great wants, fitte to be forgiuen in so reuerend antiquity. (*Apologie for Poetrie.*)
> *Webbe:* the manner of hys stile may seeme blunte and course to many fine Englishe eares at these dayes.
> *Ascham:* [is very reserved in *The Scholemaster* but in *Toxophilus* he calls Chaucer 'our English Homer'.]
> *Chapman:* Chaucer (by whom we will needes authorise our true english) had more new wordes for his time then any man needes to devise now.

(a)   Who comments on Chaucer's language?

(b)   Who calls him an example to later poets?

(c) Who complains of his shortcomings? And what are these shortcomings?

(a) Sidney, Webbe, Chapman.

(b) Gascoigne, Sidney, Chapman.

(c) Sidney, Webbe.

I hope you felt that Webbe's strictures weren't really enough evidence for an answer. What does he mean by 'blunte and course'? Clearly not the *Knight's Tale*. Although he refers to 'stile', he may also object to subject. For some Elizabethans, Chaucer's bawdy was meat too strong. Harington defended Ariosto by saying that Chaucer was worse: he 'incurreth far more the reprehension of flat scurrilitie . . . not onely in his millers tale, but in the good wife of Bathes tale, & many more'. The answer is that it's not possible to be absolutely sure what Webbe and Sidney were objecting to. Ascham deplored his use of rhyme, but praised him none the less (see above). That is as explicit as anything we get. Elizabethan critics have a maddening habit of not supporting their generalizations with illustration; take heed! With a conscious plan of reforming the language themselves, they admired Chaucer's attempts to polish and refine with a leaven of French words the unsophisticated English tongue. They condemned him for not going far enough. Look again at the *Knight's Tale* passage. Is there anything there that might not seem sufficiently polished to an Elizabethan who admired ornate language?

It's a question of degree, I think. An Elizabethan poet tackling the same subject and with the same attitudes would not have restricted himself to Chaucer's simple epithets, but would have constructed far more sophisticated ornaments.

3.3 We have already met one of the basic principles that Elizabethan poets conscientiously set themselves to follow: decorum, or the proper fitting of style to subject. It was itself a principle derived from classical theory. Ascham's words on the subject (from *The Scholemaster*) sound like a cry from the heart:

> Ye know not what hurt ye do to learning, that care not for wordes but for matter, and so make a deuorse betwixt the tong and the hart.

Style was not considered less important than subject: the ideal was a proper marriage between them. In the television programme that accompanies these two units you will see how ornament in all things was a striking feature of the Elizabethan Court circle. Poetry was not excepted. Nevertheless, standards of taste did apply, and monstrosities were despised. George Puttenham devoted a third of his *Arte of English Poesie* to a discussion of the types and proper use of ornament in poetry:

> Ornament . . . is of two sortes; one to satisfie & delight th'eare only by a goodly outward shew set upon the matter with wordes and speaches smothly and tunably running, another by certaine intendments or sence of such wordes & speaches inwardly working a stirre to the mynde.

Puttenham does not despise either of these kinds: make sure you understand what he means, because I shall be returning to them later. Too much ornament would mean that a subject appeared artificially inflated out of all proportion to its importance. This was as much despised as no attention to style at all:

The high stile is disgraced and made foolish and ridiculous by all wordes affected, counterfait, and puffed up, as it were a windball carrying more countenance than matter, and cannot be better resembled then to these midsummer pageants in London, where, to make the people wonder, are set forth great and vglie Gyants marching as if they were aliue, and armed at all points, but within they are stuffed full of browne paper and tow, which the shrewd boyes underpeering do guilefully discover and turne to a great derision.

Puttenham: *The Arte of English Poesie.*

In the following brief extract from Shakespeare's *Love's Labours Lost* Don Armado ('a fantastical Spaniard') and Holofernes (a schoolmaster and pedant) vie with one another in the high-falutin'-ness of their language:

Armado: Sir, it is the king's most sweet pleasure and affection to congratulate the princess at her pavilion in the posteriors of this day. Which the rude multitude call the afternoon.

Holofernes: The posterior of the day, most generous sir, is liable, congruent, and measurable for the afternoon: the word is well culled, chose; sweet and apt, I do assure you, sir; I do assure.

Love's Labours Lost, V. i. 79–86, ed. Richard David, Arden edition, Methuen, 1968.

And if you know *Hamlet,* you will remember Osric, own brother to Armado in verbal affectation. In them over-refinement of style has become comic. But of course, these are extreme instances, and because you will be dealing for the most part with the best of the age in these units, you are not likely to meet such exaggeration. Decorum is really a question of taste. For example, a poet with a lady to persuade will quite fittingly try all the tricks of wit and flowery language to charm her – and block her retreat. But a poem sincerely praising chastity, or a devotional poem, demands a less sophisticated, more obviously serious style. A poem that condemns will use plainer language than one which praises or flatters. A martial subject demands sternness, and light wit in such a case would be out of place. In the poems in the following section and subsequently, keep an eye open to see if this fundamental principle is being observed.

4.0 PRACTICAL CRITICISM OF LYRIC POETRY

4.1 Now I want to leave theory for the time being, and look at practice. We are also moving from long poems to short ones.

Read carefully the following poems. They are a mixed bunch, some of them amongst the finest short Elizabethan poems, some far less distinguished. For the most part, they are simpler than the poems you will be studying in the next unit, so use this extended exercise to limber up, and exercise your skills in criticizing a poetic text.

(i) Anon: *Thule, the period of cosmography* (p. 28)

(ii) A. W.: *Smooth are thy looks* (p. 34)

(iii) Campion: *When thou must home* (p. 58)

(iv) Drayton: *Since there's no help* (p. 106)

(v) Gascoigne: *And if I did, what then?* (p. 122)

(vi) Greville: *I, with whose colours Myra dressed her head* (p. 137)

(vii)   Marlowe: *The passionate shepherd to his love* (Additional Poems 3)

(viii) Percy: *It shall be said I died for Coelia!* (p. 207)

(ix)   Raleigh: *The nymph's reply* (Additional Poems 4)

(x)   Sidney: *Fly, fly my friends* (p. 237)

(xi)   Spenser: *One day I wrote her name upon the strand* (p. 250)

Take each poem in turn, and in your notebooks *first* try to sum up in a phrase or two what the poem is about; *second*, try to define the mood or tone of the poem; *third*, make some remarks on the style of presentation of the piece. Sometimes deciding what the subject is will involve making up your mind what the imagery refers to. Tone can be difficult to define, but you may find that it helps you to read the poem aloud, acting the piece; see what mood the poem needs to be said in. Keep this bit brief, and justify your choice of words (if need be) in the 'style' section. If it is relevant, you should also comment on whether the poet 'keeps decorum'. I want you to do your own ground-work on these poems, but before you begin, it would be as well to introduce those of you for whom this is an entirely new field to two common Elizabethan fictions in poetry: the *pastoral* and *courtly love* conventions.

Pastoralism

Like Marie Antoinette at Versailles, the Elizabethans occasionally liked to imagine that they were shepherds and shepherdesses. However, with a stronger sense of reality, they seldom did more than pretend in verse and song: dressing up they left to actors. The pastoral world of the poets was a never-never land where all your sheep were pretty lambs. If the shepherd was sad, all nature hung its head; if his suit to his shepherdess was going well, the flowers bloomed. Or the poet could choose to draw a contrast between the wretchedness of the love-lorn shepherd and the indifference of the rest of creation: look at *Lodge*'s *The earth, late choked with showers* (p. 171) which, although it doesn't mention shepherds, has the simplistic pastoral view of nature.

Courtly love

This was really a survival from the Middle Ages. In twelfth-century France, where the custom began, the Lady of the court was often the only well-born lady whom the young knights of her Lord's entourage could dedicate their deeds to. Virtuous and valorous deeds done in her name would enhance the lady's glory and might win her praise, even her love. She was mistress because her suitor was her servant, and at her mercy for a smile or a kiss. By Elizabeth's reign much of the convention was no more than a game which the Queen herself liked to play, but nevertheless, the ideal of the 'verray parfit gentil knight' (Chaucer's words) persisted. You will meet both these conventions in the poems I have selected for your close attention.

What follows is not by any means a complete account of each poem. But if your notes miss any of my points, be sure to go back to the poem and check whether you agree with me. If you have noticed something I have omitted, you may well be right, of course: but check up on yourself very scrupulously.

(i) Anon: *Thule, the period of cosmography* The poet compares his own paradoxical state in love with the wonders of the world.

Tone: bombastic, self-applauding.

Style: the poem is completely overwhelmed by its imagery, which is on
such a scale that the last two lines of each stanza sound bathetic in
contrast. This looks to me like a breach of decorum, but it had its
admirers among contemporaries. Do you remember Thomas Weelkes's
setting which you heard on the music record for this course? The poet
has tried for a high style, but seems to have overreached himself.
However, if you felt that 'fry' was a very bathetic word, look at Southwell's poem *The burning babe* (p. 245) where you will see it in an
umistakably serious context.

(ii) A.W.: *Smooth are thy looks* Although he knows her beauty hides cruelty,
he has to love her.

Tone: confident and sophisticated, though slightly abject in places –
'And like to kiss the lips that fret my life.'

Style: there are traces of the servant–mistress courtly love relationship
here. The lady is clearly setting the pace. The sound is predominantly
soft – note the number of soft 's' sounds in the first five lines. What
surprises there are, are not strident. 'Swallowing' in line 2 is unexpected,
and effective. 'Fretted' suggests both kissing ('fret' meaning 'to gnaw')
and the fretfulness that followed. There is almost a pun there, as in
the two senses of 'heat' in line 15. A carefully arranged pattern of
opposites arranged in a witty paradox; the patterning is particularly
obvious in that the first words of the first four lines are repeated in the
fifth, and followed by their opposites in the sixth.

(iii) Campion: *When thou must home* He imagines the lady he loves in vain
recounting her triumphs in the after-life.

Tone: quiet, melancholy, urbane.

Style: Polished smooth, fairly low-key: 'home', 'finished'. Classical and
courtly references. The 'point' carefully reserved for the last line, but
artfully anticipated in line 6.

(iv) Drayton: *Since there's no help* The end of a love-affair which he would
like to revive.

Tone: virile, ironic, genuine. It is partly the tonal modulations of this
poem that make it so great.

Style: a sonnet – see Section 2.2. It is divided regularly into three
quatrains and a couplet, with a distinct break in sense after the second.
The sestet contains many of the traditional aspects of the forsaken
courtly lover's complaint, but the realism of the octet casts an ironic
colouring on to the fantasy of lines 9–12, and suggests very dramatically
a man who dislikes emotion trying to hide his real feelings by exaggerating
them.

(v) Gascoigne: *And if I did, what then?* Staggered by his mistress's airy
confession of infidelity, he contemplates his ridiculous situation.

Tone: Flabbergasted, turning to wry 'let them wait'.

Style: Like Drayton's sonnet, semi-dramatic – you can almost hear the
other voice in the dialogue. The brisk metre helps suggest that this
lover is not taking himself too seriously. The language ('popped a
question') and imagery (fishing) down-to-earth. 'Low' style, which
very much 'keeps decorum' with the poet's subject and attitude.

(vi) Greville: *I with whose colours Myra dressed her head* The structure of each verse retells the story: the first four lines describe how she once loved him, the last couplet makes it clear that she has been untrue, though he still loves her.

Tone: quite tough and reasonable; angry, but not harsh.

Style: a syntactical break after stanza 3. Stanzas 1–3: a catalogue of the gifts and confidences they exchanged, brought together in stanza 3, just as in A.W.'s poem the lady's attributes are given a line each (1–4) and tied together in line 5. A bit of a mixture: classical references in stanza 4, and rather self-conscious conceits in stanza 3 line 3, stanza 5, line 2; but some unaffected, homely words – stanza 1, line 3, and 'mad girls'. I hope you liked this one!

(vii) Marlowe: *The passionate shepherd to his love* He promises her all kinds of country delights if she will live with him.

Tone: confident, winning.

Style: this makes me almost wish the pastoral fantasy were true! Swift, but lingering on lovely details. No metaphors – the poem is beautiful because of quite solid-seeming things, not images. No obsessive patterning, just enough link between the beginning ('Come live . . .') and the last two stanzas. This poem can trace its family tree back to Catullus's 'Vivamus, mea Lesbia, atque amemus.'

(viii) Percy: *It shall be said I died for Coelia* The punishments he feels he deserves for wasting his attentions on an unresponsive lady are (he implies) made worthwhile by the fame he will achieve as a constant lover.

Tone: crazy? masochistic?

Style: another sonnet – three quatrains and a couplet. The rejected courtly lover again – I hope you're not getting tired of him. What you should be noticing is that each poet taking up a very common theme is forced to find some new way of treating it. He often isolates some novel incongruity or paradox, and in a poem like this a sense of terrific strain is apparent. Again, classical paraphernalia. Very unoriginal epithets – 'grisly man', 'liquid air', 'dark clouds', 'everlasting ire'.

(ix) Raleigh: *The nymph's reply* (I hope you realized which other poem this is a reply to! It's not quite certain that the author is Raleigh, but he was a friend of Marlowe's.) The shepherd's temporal inducements could only move her if youth lasted for ever.
(In Catullus's poem which began this tradition, it was death, not old age, which the poet feared.)

Tone: stern, but wonderfully wistful in the last stanza.

Style: of course, the poem takes most of its cues from Marlowe's poem, but whereas the things that Marlowe described had a beauty all their own, Raleigh refers to them figuratively with extra words implying a moral judgement (stanzas 3, 4, 5).

(x) Sidney: *Fly, fly my friends* A lady looked at him, and he fell in love.

Tone: energetic, conversational and ironic.

Style: wittily hyperbolical. The metaphor is an impossible fiction – even grotesque: Cupid is in ambush behind a lady's eyelashes. (Notice that this is a very 'modern' Cupid with bullets replacing bow and arrow!) But we've met hyperbole before where it wasn't meant to be amusing. Here, I'm convinced it is. The seriousness of the first line is put in doubt by the breathless conversational tone of the second line. The anger isn't wrath – it's exasperation – notice such 'clipped' expressions as 'in dark bush' (no article), 'bloody bullet', 'Nor so fair level in so secret stay'. There's a manly understatement in line 10 which makes a nice change from the more common abject attitudes of the lover. Yet Sidney maintains his independent irony within an entirely conventional poetic situation: Cupid deals the blow; a glance from a lady's eye is fatal. Again, this is a sonnet, divided into two quatrains and a sestet.

(xi)   Spenser: *One day I wrote her name upon the strand*   He claims that his poetry will make her virtues and their love live for ever.

Tone: Cool, philosophical, contemplative – hardly emotional.

Style: very plain and stately; even harsh in places – 'wiped out'. Are the first four lines an image or an anecdote? The very austerity of the situation invites you to ask whether writing in the sand is a metaphor for writing love poetry. The crescendo comes in lines 11–12, where the verse moves towards hyperbole, and the sole unmistakable image of the poem. Like many serious poets, Spenser was troubled with the thought that he ought to pick a worthier subject than ordinary human love. Spenser is trying to see the human element in the context of all spiritual love.

4.2   Love, the subject of all these poems, is one of the most common of human experiences – but no one ever wants to admit this. Hence the sometimes frantic search for novel imagery to describe it. Turn back to Section 3.3 and the quotation from Puttenham: 'Ornament is of two sorts'. Which sort has A.W. aimed at? And which sort best describes Greville's effects, especially the first two lines of the last stanza?

DISCUSSION

I deliberately worded those questions badly. I hope you answered that really both poets were trying to achieve both sorts of effect. Neither wants to be unpleasing to the ear, and both want to effect a 'stirre to the mynde'. However, I think that A.W. pays more attention to the former, Greville to the latter. It is Puttenham's second kind which is more interesting. Elizabethan poets wanted to surprise their readers into a belief that their love was unique; they wanted to flatter the lady in the case into a belief that *she* was unique. And so Greville claims that Myra is so white that she washes the water she bathes in – whiteness like the Queen's famous pale complexion being an ideal of beauty then. A mind-teasing image like that would be praised as 'witty' or 'ingenious'; it was sometimes called a 'conceit' – though the term is more common in the seventeenth century. Of course, such figures had their dangers. I expect you sometimes felt that a poet's inspiration was not his love but his bright idea. A similar amount of effort goes into the choice and arrangement of words. Many of these poems are artefacts, craftsman's pieces, well made and nicely finished, but without much true vitality.

But not all the poems we have looked at exist on the surface alone. Look at Drayton's and Sidney's sonnets. What are they reacting against?

DISCUSSION

Fictions and extravagances. Yet both mock the convention of a love that consists of words alone *from within* (see initial discussion of both poems). Now look again at Gascoigne's poem, and the other two in the Anthology: *The lullaby of a lover* (p. 120) and *The green knight's farewell to fancy* (p. 123). Gascoigne rejects the whole fiction of the courtly lover – but he does not use its language to do so. In the first he admits good-humouredly that he is too old for all that nonsense (Robin is a common Elizabethan nickname for the phallus); in the third there is more bitterness in his tone and he rejects not only the whole artificial world of the court and its culture, but its rural alternative as well, under the general name of Fancy. I like both poems enormously because they present simultaneously his present feeling and what he has left behind: look for example at the last verse of *The lullaby* and the third verse of *The farewell*.

4.3   Many critics have noticed that alongside the rich stream of ornate poetry there runs a thin, but distinct current of a simpler, cooler kind. C. S. Lewis called the strains the 'golden and the drab' – a distinction which implies the condemnation of one kind. But do you like Gascoigne any less than you like, say, Sidney's sonnet?

Well, perhaps you do. I don't. Turn to *Raleigh's* poem *The lie* (p. 210). Do you think Lewis would have called this poem golden or drab?

DISCUSSION

There is so little ornament in it that the answer must be drab – and yet I find the poem very interesting. As you may know, the courtier's life was precarious, and Raleigh's was no exception. The poem seems to speak to us very directly out of his bitterness at being banished from the court he loved so much. Significantly, his most ornamental poems are the verses he addressed to the Queen when trying to regain her favour and his place at court. Normally, the baroque element in his poetry is tempered by a sense of life's seriousness. Look at *Nature that washed her hands in milk* (p. 213). Here the imagery is novel enough to effect a 'stirre to the mynde' – but the solemn almost monosyllabic plainness of the last verse is anticipated by the strain of simplicity throughout: 'And had forgot to dry them'. I find a similar duality in *The passionate man's pilgrimage* (p. 208). Note your reactions to this poem.

DISCUSSION

I'm aware that you may find this just too much – the 'crystal buckets' for example. But for me it's precisely this rather naïve acceptance of the imagery of *The Book of Revelation* which makes the poem so interesting: you cannot separate it from the terrible clear vision of his own execution which ends the poem. Simplicity here is the humility of the pilgrim, a surrender of the will and intellect to God, a refusal of the fashionable, worldly, witty way. Once again, drab is a word I should be very reluctant to use of Raleigh.

4.4   To conclude this section, I want to tie up these two strains with the two voices we identified in Chaucer. This is a matter in debate amongst scholars, so you do not have to take my word for it. But Chaucer uses his more ornate language to describe Emily, heroine of *The Knight's Tale, locus classicus* of the chivalric code. The Elizabethan poets who favoured a similar style tried to live by the same code; their language is as mannered as the culture of their court. Pandarus on the other hand has less time for pretty manners in love. And the Elizabethans who prefer an equal plain bluff style are those who are rejecting or criticizing the values of the courtly life. In a poem like *The passionate man's pilgrimage* the repudiation is not obvious, but it's implied: Raleigh has rejected the secular world. Broadly speaking, the plain style is the language of protest.

5.0   EDMUND SPENSER

5.1   *Edmund Spenser* (1552?–99) is the greatest and most typical of Elizabethan poets, but he is not necessarily the one you will enjoy most: Milton called him 'our sage and serious poet'.

He was educated at the new Merchant Taylor's School where his headmaster's firm belief 'Our language is capable if our people will be painful' – i.e. diligent (see Section 1.2) must have influenced the boy. There he was trained in the classics, and his first publications were verse translations from the French. At Cambridge he met Gabriel Harvey, an ardent supporter of quantitative metres; Spenser made the experiment (p. 262 of your set book) but was not convinced.

After university he went to London, where from 1578 he was in the service of the Earl of Leicester, leader of the Puritan party which felt itself specially threatened by a possible marriage between the Queen and the Duke of Alençon. From this point on, he was politically in the thick of things. Like most Elizabethans he was not just a poet.

In 1579, he published *The Shepheardes Calender*, a long pastoral poem of a more sombre colouring than Marlowe's *Passionate Shepherd*, full of disguised references to political and religious controversies of his time. Vergil's first important poems had been his pastoral *Eclogues*, and Spenser's work expresses classical forms in a language which owes much to Chaucer. We shall not look at it, but note that his contemporaries immediately recognized its great promise: Sidney said that it was one of the very few English poems to have 'poetical sinews in them' (*Troilus and Criseyde* was another); and Webbe proclaimed 'now yet at the last hath England hatched up one poet . . . comparable with the best in any respect'.

In 1580 Spenser was appointed secretary to Elizabeth's Governor of Ireland, Lord Grey of Wilton, and spent much of the rest of his life in that country. He loved the landscape, but was disgusted with the poverty and violence of the people – Ireland was an uncomfortably close breeding ground of Catholic menace to Protestant England. But Spenser had been educated to believe that all knowledge must be put to some useful purpose, and so he wrote (about 1595) *A View of the Present State of Ireland*, which was circulated, but considered too radical to be printed.

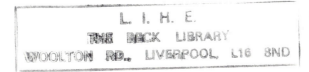

In Ireland Spenser met Raleigh, chief favourite of the 1580s, who introduced the poet and the first three books of his *Faerie Queene* to the Queen, herself the Gloriana of his poem to whom all the knights were to pay tribute. Other poems of the late '80s and '90s are *Colin Clouts come home again* (his pastoral name for himself); the sonnet sequence *Amoretti*, and the two marriage poems – extracts from which are in your anthology. The next three books of *The Faerie Queene* were published in 1596.

He started his great allegorical poem in about 1580, and did not live to complete more than six of the projected twelve books. We can see something of his plans for the whole from his prefatory letter to Raleigh. His hero was Arthur, 'the image of a brave knight, perfected in the twelve private moral vertues'. In practice, each book has a virtue and a knightly hero to embody or defend it, and Arthur, embodying all the virtues under the general name of 'magnificence' intervenes at the moment of each virtue's supreme test. Book I is the legend of the Red Cross Knight, or Holiness; Book II Sir Guyon or Temperance: Book III Britomart (a female knight) or Chastity – and so on. We shall be paying special attention to an episode in Book II, where Sir Guyon helped by a Palmer, or pilgrim (see Raleigh's poem) who guides him in his quest, destroys the Bower of Bliss and its wicked occupant, the witch Acrasia, who has already killed the knight Mordant and his wife Amavia. Milton calls Spenser 'a better teacher than Scotus or Aquinas, describing true temperance under the person of Guion, [and] brings him in with his palmer through the cave of Mammon and the bower of earthly bliss, that he might see and know and yet abstain'.

5.2   Now read the three sonnets and the extract from *An hymn of heavenly love* in your anthology. Does the love in the former have anything to do with the love in the latter? Comment briefly.

Then read *Prothalamion* (p. 251), a more decorative, celebratory poem. There is a 'conceit' in it similar to one you have met already in a poem by Greville: can you find it? And what is the effect of the motif of the river and the swans in a bridal song?

DISCUSSION

Love in Spenser is never wholly eros; it always contains some element of agape. If it does not, it is not love at all, but lust. If you didn't understand that, you'd better revise the section on *neo-Platonism* in Units 5–6. Ficino thought *all* love an aspiration to the perfect beauty which was God. In the Hymn, the heavenly creative power (the Craftsman, or Demiurge), is Love whose son (stanza 2) is an ideal human love; the trinity is completed by an incomprehensible spiritual love. Finally, the ultimate creating love is seen as the source of the power which might infuse his poetry. This poem is filled with one of the most basic of neo-Platonic principles, which sees all degrees of energy as part of the same chain of force. In the sonnet *Let not one spark* (p. 251) the energy of the poem is concentrated in the idea of the pure and transcendent love she deserves. The second sonnet we have looked at already. The first exalts a milder love above the thrills of the chase. Perhaps we cannot call them explicitly neo-Platonic, but in all of them physical love vies with spirituality.

In *Prothalamion* the swans are thought of as whiter than the stream in stanza 3, but the conceit here is not just a pretty compliment. Whiteness and purity are integral concepts of this poem. Water, or a river, is traditionally associated with fertility and marriage, but in Spenser's poem the limpid Thames with its white swans also serves to temper carnality. Even the flowers (stanza 2) are predominantly pale. Look at stanza 4: 'the swans' seem to be of 'angels' breed' though really 'bred of summer's heat'; yet that heat is tempered by the word 'fresh', repeated twice. This is the ideal for the lovers whose wedding the poem celebrates: their natural heat should resemble the purest spiritual beauty.

5.3   Now read the extract from *Faerie Queene* Book II – *The Bower of Bliss* (Additional Poems 5). Each stanza of the *Faerie Queene* has eight lines of ten syllables, and a last line of twelve. I hope you noticed the beauty of *Prothalamion's* metre: the *Faerie Queene* stanza is less showy, but can achieve extraordinary grace. Comment on the effects of the long last line in stanzas 70, 74, 78, 80, 87.

DISCUSSION

70: sums up the whole stanza, and in its own musicality, reflects what the stanza is about. 74: sound echoing sense – the 'a' of 'falles' less distinct than that of 'fades'. 78: the break (cesura) comes late in the line – the extra length of these last lines is both reassuringly regular, and capable of great variety. 80: it can be used for emphatic moral comment. 87: it is really the only place in any stanza where anything dramatic in the narrative can happen.

In each stanza there are only three rhymes (ababbcbcc), which demanded a vocabulary wider than some would have admitted possible in the English of the time. Spenser enlarged his vocabulary in two ways: by making up new words (coinages) and by reviving old ones (archaisms). Of course, he did not use his new words only for rhymes: for example, 'attune' (76) is never recorded prior to this. In stanza 78 he revives the old meaning of 'thrild' which is 'pierced', and 'dight' (77) meaning 'dressed for' was obsolescent when Spenser revived it. He was probably attracted to old words out of his admiration for Chaucer and because of the nature of his subject – chivalric antiquity. (For a hostile comment on this practice, see Daniel's *Let others sing*.)

5.4   I hope this passage reminded you of Fairfax's Tasso and Harington's Ariosto, because in their original Italian both the passages you read were amongst Spenser's sources. Remember that although (as we have seen) originality of detail was important to the Elizabethans, originality of plot was not likely to rank very highly in a literary climate where the imitation of established masters was the duty of every aspiring poet. Spenser copies several lines in this passage directly from Tasso.

Compare this passage with the Tasso, where Armida, like Acrasia, is an enchantress. What is the most important difference between the two passages, and what does this suggest?

DISCUSSION

Spenser omits the mirror, which in Tasso symbolizes the mutual (reflected) love of Rinaldo and Armida. His Verdant is a helpless victim. This suggests that Spenser has a more solemn purpose than Tasso, who is more concerned with the pleasures of sensuality than with moral discrimination – his comment in stanza 3 line 5 is very brief. But Armida's love is genuine, and her sensuality is therefore permissible. Acrasia does not love Verdant; her sensuality is totally depraved.

5.5   What is this moral purpose, and how is it expressed? First, read stanzas 83–end again. What is the literary archetype of these men transformed into beasts? (There's a clue in the Chapman passage if you need one.)

DISCUSSION

Circe, the Sorceress in the *Odyssey*, transformed many of Ulysses' men into beasts. As you know, from the Middle Ages the classics had been 'moralized', and allegories of vice and virtue made out of their narratives. The story of Circe was read as a warning that sensual indulgence can reduce a man to a beast. But Verdant has not reached that stage – yet. Read stanzas 79–80 again. What state of degradation has Verdant reached? Underline the words which indicate Spenser's disapproval. And look carefully at Botticelli's *Mars and Venus*. Do you see any connection?

Figure 1   Botticelli: Mars and Venus (*The National Gallery*)

DISCUSSION

Spenser's disapproval is indicated in the words 'great pittie'; 'foule deface'; 'Yet sleeping'; 'idel'; 'sleeping praise'; 'fowly ra'st'; 'ne for honour cared he' etc. A knight, whose prime business is vigilance, lies sleeping, his armour abandoned. His vulnerability is culpable. He is poised between the dignity of a man and brutishness – not yet an animal, yet without the attributes which raise a man above his animal nature.

I hope your earlier work on allegory and Florentine art enabled you to see that Botticelli's picture has a moral significance too. The story of Mars and Venus was (traditionally) made morally edifying by interpreting it as the subjugation of warlike passions by love (cf. Greene's poem, p. 135). Now Botticelli's Venus is clearly *agape*, not *eros*; Spenser's Acrasia is the other side of the coin. Botticelli's Venus looks beyond her lover: the world is in her clear and steady gaze. But Acrasia hangs over Verdant like a spider, her attention concentrated on her victim (73). One of the features of neo-Platonic thinking is the closeness of opposites. Vice readily suggests its corresponding virtue, and virtue its forbidden opposite. Spenser uses the traditional interpretation of Mars and Venus to suggest its opposite, but his reader would be aware of his contrasting starting-point.

But if Spenser meant Acrasia to appear wicked, why did he make the description of the Bower so beautiful? Read the song (stanzas 74–5). If this were out of context would anything suggest that Spenser's purpose was not the praise of sensual love?

DISCUSSION

The song follows the traditional theme 'carpe diem' – 'seize the day' (Horace, *Odes* I xi); or rather, 'carpe florem' (Ovid) – 'pluck the flower' – a more specific invitation to the pleasures of sex. The flower in bud is a conventional symbol of virginity; the blown rose a warning of the speed with which youth vanishes. (Transitoriness was a favourite theme of the Elizabethans – look at Barnes's lovely sonnet *A blast of wind*, p. 42.) Only the last word of these two stanzas makes Spenser's purpose unmistakably plain, but is he really demanding more moral alertness in his reader than that? What about 'bold and free'; 'bared bosome'; 'broad display'? Seductively sensual, and not the way of chastity. The reader's moral obliviousness may repeat Verdant's fall. But perhaps like an Elizabethan reader, you were sufficiently attuned not to be misled. Just as Acrasia leans over her victim, so the song looks narrowly towards the transitory, earthly pleasures of sex, and not towards any permanent good.

5.6 The expectation that poetry should be a vehicle for 'doctrine' lay at the heart of any serious Elizabethan poet's defence of his art. But of course he wanted to please as well. In order to fulfil the conventional design of pleasure with instruction, Spenser chose to write 'a continued allegory or darke conceit'.

> The generall end . . . of all the booke is to fashion a gentleman or noble person in vertuous and gentle discipline: Whiche for that I conceiued shoulde be most plausible and pleasing, being coloured with an historicall fiction, the which the most part of men delight to read, rather for variety of matter, then for profit of the ensample . . . To some I know this Methode will seem displeasaunt, which had rather have good discipline deliuered plainly in way of precepts, or sermoned at large, as they vse, then thus clowdily enwrapped in Allegoricall deuices. But . . . all things (are) accounted by their showes, and nothing esteemed of, that is not delightfull and pleasing to commune sence.
>
> *Prefatory letter to Ralegh.*

You have already been introduced to medieval allegory – biblical exegesis and the moralizing of the classics (Units 5–6). Renaissance allegory was, if anything, even more engrossing, and the iconographic element in it was in no way diminished.

93   *Temperantia.*

HEERE *Temperance* I ftand, of virtues, Queene,
     Who moderate all humane vaine defires,
Wherefore a bridle in my hand is feene,
To curbe affection, that too farre afpires:
    I'th other hand, that golden cup doth fhow,
    Vnto exceffe I am a deadly foe.

For when to luftes, I loofely let the raine,
And yeeld to each fuggefting appetite,
Man to his ruine, headlong runnes amaine,
To frendes great greife, and enimies delight:
    No conqueft doubtles, may with that compare,
    Of our affectes, when we the victors are.

            Quæ rego virtutes placido moderamine cunctas
              Affectufque potens fum Dea SOPHROSYNE:
            Effrænes animi doceo cohibere furores,
              Suftineo, abftineo, difplicet omne nimis.

        Nihil eft tam præclarum, tamque magnificum, quod non moderatione

*Figure 2   Temperantia: from
Henry Peacham,* Minerva
Brittana *1612 (p. 93)*
(*The British Museum*)

This kind of allegory is traditional and so simple as to be almost commonplace. Now, as we have already seen, Spenser's allegory is not simple, but it does contain traditional elements. Is there anything in Peacham's *Temperantia* which might explain why Guyon, the knight of Temperance, apparently behaves so intemperately in his destruction of the Bower? For a fuller discussion of this kind of allegory, see Unit 20, Section 2.

DISCUSSION

The line 'Unto excesse I am a *deadly* foe'. Guyon's rampage also seems psychologically plausible: he is over-reacting to the concealed treachery of the Bower – perhaps tacitly admitting that he too was stirred by its apparent beauty. Though of course I would not have expected you to be able to prove this, Spenser tells us a few stanzas before your extract begins that Guyon's 'stubborne brest gan secret pleasaunce to embrace'.

Guyon is the Knight of Temperance, but he needs a helper. What do you think the Palmer stands for? And what qualities are allegorized in Acrasia and Verdant?

DISCUSSION

I hope you felt that this is not the kind of allegory which translates into simple abstractions. The Palmer guides the actions of Temperance, and has been called Reason – but this takes no account of his character as a Pilgrim who had been to the Holy Land. Perhaps we could say that to Guyon the Palmer is some kind of vision of holy ends. If you called Acrasia Sexual Intemperance you would be right of course – but you would be simplifying Spenser's allegory. Sexual Intemperance sounds ugly, and Acrasia seems beautiful. An allegorical interpretation must make sense of the whole narration. Verdant is complex too. Quite literally he is green, and dangerously ready for Acrasia's snares. He represents a crisis in a young man's life. There comes a point where we must ask ourselves whether, if we cannot give an exact name to Spenser's moral abstractions, they are really allegories in any meaningful sense of the word. If Acrasia were a calculating, experienced 'older woman' in a novel, and Verdant, say, a bemused young poet, we should recognize that both characters embodied moral qualities and measure them against generalities. But we shouldn't call it allegory. Why then do we unfalteringly call what Spenser writes allegory? Write your comments.

DISCUSSION

I think it's a question of degree. A novelist generally makes a gesture towards realism, and does not subordinate his whole world to his moral purposes. And yet can we say that even Spenser makes every detail of the Bower confirm its innate evil to the wary reader? Look at stanza 71. Does anything there indicate the nature of its inhabitants? Perhaps Spenser wanted to suggest that nature may be an innocent accomplice of Intemperance. I leave you to think further on the subject.

5.7 To conclude, look at a virtuous garden – *The garden of Adonis* (p. 258), and answer these questions. How do you know from the first two stanzas that this is a 'good' garden? What sort of love does Venus here represent, and what does Adonis stand for?

DISCUSSION

The first two stanzas set the tone of the whole passage by concentrating on the free and unrestricted growth of Nature without Art ('sharp steel did never lop'; 'not by art, But by the trees' own inclination made') which shelters the garden from extremes of heat and cold. Also, the flowers in the Bower are completely sterile; but the garden is 'fruitful'. The fifth stanza is difficult. Book III is the book of Chastity, but it would be wrong to think that Venus is unchaste – stanza 5 proves it. Venus cannot be evil because of the nature of her Adonis. I hope that you spotted the neo-Platonic references: Adonis is 'Father of all forms' – the craftsman or Demiurge 'that living gives to all'. Spenser, still following Ficino, unites this creativity to Venus, who here is *eros*, rather than *agape*. We should notice that the love between them is truly mutual ('Joying his goddess, and of her enjoyed') unlike that of Acrasia and Verdant.

Spenser died in the last year of the century; Elizabeth was old and soon to die herself. The only contemporary allusion to the poet's death is a letter written four days afterwards: 'Spenser, our principal poet, coming lately out of Ireland, died at Westminster on Saturday last' – the very casualness of that reference to him as 'our principal poet' is a clear indication of the secure regard in which he was held. We know from later accounts that his funeral was attended by poets and noblemen, who threw elegies into his open grave.

His achievement was that he had taken all the elements available to poets of his time, and, following their common precepts, united them into something new and unique. He combines moral profundity and learning with beauty of expression; respect for the ancients with love for his own native tradition; a joy in the power of his language with a discreet ear for extravagance. With Spenser, English poetry can be said to have arrived.

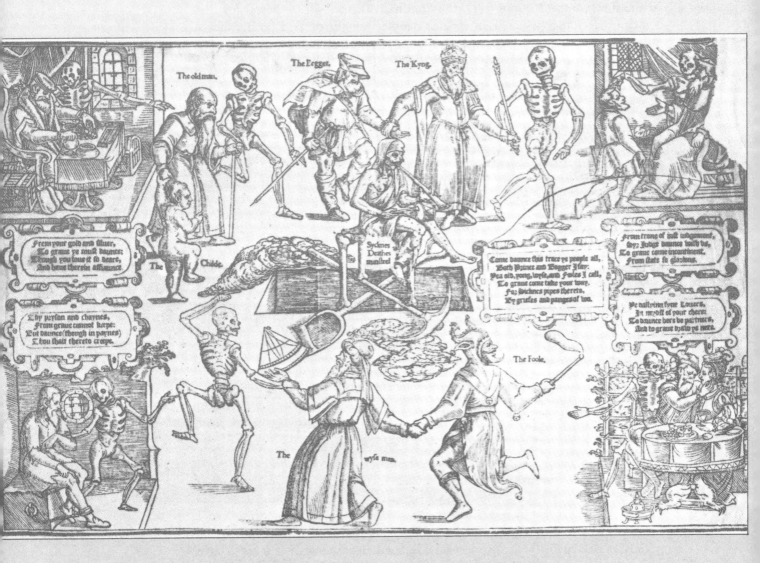

Panorama of the Dance and Song of Death: a broadside woodcut from about 1569.

1.0   INTRODUCTION

1.1   In this week's work, having spent your first week of study on Elizabethan poetry mainly on matters of theory and style, and having, we hope, developed a feeling for the genre as well as a way of looking at poetry, you will briefly consider some of the standard thinking about the problems of achieving decorum in poetry that we find among Elizabethan poets; and then study a further selection of Elizabethan poetry, mainly from *The Penguin Book of Elizabethan Verse*. Some additional poems essential to my purpose have been included in this text and at the end of it, and I have also referred, occasionally, both to other poems and to whole poems of which extracts only are included in this text and in your set book. You are not required to follow up these references to material outside the study unit and the set text.

By way of introduction, I discuss in Section 2 Elizabethan attitudes to the making of poetry, and the decay of allegory.

Thereafter, the poems for study will be grouped under three headings and treated thematically; though you will appreciate that there is bound to be some overlapping, as well as inclusion of other subject matter.

1.2   In the first group (Sections 3–4), the dominant theme will be *Mutability*, the principle of change which Renaissance people thought of as a positive force built into the working of nature. Do not expect the poets to be as exact as historians of ideas or philosophers ought to be; expect them rather to make their own syntheses of existing systems of knowledge and belief, and to apply them, usually in metaphorical ways, to their own poetic purpose. We know that Spenser had read Plato and some of the neo-Platonists, and was aware of how the doctrine of the Forms could be applied to the problem of Mutability; and we can also see in his poetry awareness of the principle of perpetual flux and the oppositions inherent in it, as advanced by Heraclitus. But above all, we appreciate from reading his poetry that he uses those classical ideas as a means of establishing his own Christian position. It so happens that the poets we shall consider deal less with the creative aspects of Mutability, such as regeneration and order, than with those relating to decay and disorder. So poems dealing with Time and Death will be studied under the general heading of Mutability, and the phenomenon of Melancholy will also be briefly considered.

1.3   In the second group of poems (Sections 5–6), I shall attempt to convey something of the importance of *Music* to Elizabethan poets and their public; music as a symbolic activity, music as a source of imagery, and music as an art so akin to poetry that the two are often mutually dependent.

1.4   In the third group (Sections 7–12), the treatment of *Love* will provide the theme. Within the field of love poetry, a new kind of consciousness begins to appear towards the end of the period; and so it is appropriate to end the week with poetry that looks forward to the next age.

1.5   Two kinds of poetry which figure quite largely in your anthology are *songs* and *satire*. The accompanying gramophone record will include songs as well as readings from the poetry. Read the songs freely, including those from the plays, as preparation; there is little on the songs in this study material, and I shouldn't like you to forget that very many of the best lyrics, which we regard mainly as poetry for speaking, were for Elizabethans the words of *songs*. I have written virtually nothing on satire here, but devote the radio programme for Unit 31 to it. The broadcasting supplement will contain introductory matter for both the gramophone record and the programme on satire.

2.0   ELIZABETHAN ATTITUDES TO THE MAKING OF POETRY; AND THE DECAY OF ALLEGORY

2.1   If you took the Arts Foundation Course, you may remember that in *Form and Meaning* (Units 15–16)[1] you concentrated, in the section on literature, on imagery, studying in particular (Section 13.2) how, towards the end of the age of Shakespeare, traditional imagery began to be extended into new fields, especially in the poetry of John Donne. I described my summary of that historical development as 'considerably over-simplified', and it is now time for you to focus more closely on the manner in which Elizabethan poetry was conceived. Some teachers encourage students to look at the achievement of a previous age in the light of our knowledge of the achievement of our own – educationally speaking, a sound process, proceeding from the known to the unknown. But unless the counters used have some common currency in both ages, the inquirer finds it hard to experience a real feeling for that previous age. Cicely Havely and I have deliberately taken the opposite point of view, and based our teaching method on the assertion that, if you want to understand an age properly, you must study it in the light of its antecedents. Hence the strictly historical approach adopted by Cicely Havely in planning your previous week's work, and the attempt by John Ferguson and myself, in Units 5–6, to make you learn and feel by experience the allegorical mode of thinking prevalent at the beginning of the Renaissance period.

2.2   Allegorical thinking depended on a broadly uniform and characteristically medieval way of looking at all things, and it weakened steadily throughout the Renaissance period, so much so that Rymer, writing on Spenser in 1674, could complain that 'it was the vice of those Times to affect superstitiously the *Allegory*; and nothing would then be current without a mystical meaning' (quoted by Rosemary Freeman, *English Emblem Books*, Chatto & Windus, 1967, p. 2). As you have seen, even at the beginning of the religious controversies out of which the Reformation came, the allegorical method of interpreting Scripture was already discredited. But in poetry it lingered on, though with changes, for three very good reasons, upon which I must now dilate.

2.3   The first reason is connected with language, the medium of poetry. 'Metaphor is deeply built into the way language grows' (*Form and Meaning*, Section 11.2). For the relation between metaphor and allegory, may I refer you to Units 5–6, Section 7.3, to which I wish to add this distinction: although allegory is in essence metaphorical, a metaphor, strictly speaking, should be *fused*, i.e. understood as identified with the subject in an almost literal or concrete way, while allegory depends on a scheme of *interpretation*. Now, the images or metaphorical creations of poets make up their whole poems, and these whole poems are also,

[1] The Open University (1971) A100 Humanities. A Foundation Course. Units 15–16 *Form and Measuring*, The Open University Press.

themselves, images of what is in their creators' minds. If your response to that idea is that, by the same argument, a theory advanced by a scientist and a doctrine advanced by a political theorist or a divine are also images of what is in their originators' minds, my reply would be that the poet is consciously an image-maker, and proceeds accordingly, with due attention to the rules of decorum in his particular art; while the scientist, the political theorist and the divine usually have no such preoccupation. Since poets must in every age assure themselves of means of image-making, we should expect Renaissance poets to develop other forms of metaphorical thinking as their attachment to formal allegory weakened.

WHAT creature thou? *Occafion I doe fhowe.*
  On whirling wheele declare why dofte thou ftande?
Bicaufe, I ftill am toffed too, and froe.
Why doeft thou houlde a rafor in thy hande?
  That men maie knowe I cut on euerie fide,
  And when I come, I armies can deuide.

But wherefore haft thou winges vppon thy feete?
To fhowe, how lighte I flie with little winde.
What meanes longe lockes before? *that fuche as meete,*
Maye houlde at firfte, when they occafion finde.
  Thy head behinde all balde, what telles it more?
  That none fhoulde houlde, that let me flippe before.

Why doeft thou ftande within an open place?
That I maye warne all people not to ftaye,
But at the firfte, occafion to imbrace,
And when fhee comes, to meete her by the waye.
  Lyfippus fo did thinke it beft to bee,
  Who did deuife mine image, as you fee.

Figure 3   Occasion: from Geoffrey Whitney, A Choice of Emblemes, 1586 (The British Museum)

2.4   The second reason has to do with the state of thinking in the Renaissance. As you have already learnt, a new and idealistic, but non-empirical, system of thought, neo-Platonism, dominated the artistic scene throughout Europe and had some effect on the religious scene. The theory of perfect form, and the idea that imitation, or copying, of that form was inherent in creative processes, whether in nature or art, strongly reinforced the habit of thinking by analogy, and by metaphor. But the further this habit proceeded away from the understood bases of medieval thought, the more complicated and the more esoteric it became. In the hands of a genius like Spenser it could achieve marvellous definition, but equally, and more characteristically, it could dwindle into a process for the production of didactic *emblems*. This process becomes more and more marked throughout the period. Emblematic thinking shows in the plays of the period, and finds its most powerful expression in the public shows of the time – the masques, triumphs, ridings and other ceremonies commissioned or demanded by royalty and nobility as essential elements in the maintenance of their power, and the projection of their image (i.e. 'image' in the modern sense, relating to publicity) before the public. Let us look at one example of a didactic emblem, and one of a triumph.

2.5   My didactic emblem is taken from Geoffrey Whitney: *A Choice of Emblemes*, 1586. All over western Europe, emblem books were popular at this time, and remained so for fifty or sixty years. Many of the emblems, like this one, derived directly from classical examples. It is interesting that, at the very time when allegory of the medieval type was in decline, classical allegory, which has been imitated from the very beginning of the Renaissance, experienced a revival. In this characteristic emblem, 'thing-representing-idea' as a thought mechanism is taken so far that the 'things' in the picture are about as remote from physical actuality as they could be, having been constructed only to make a picture out of the thought upon which both poem and picture are based. You will see clearly, when you work out in detail the correspondence between the picture and the poem, that realism is no part of the emblemist's intention. Spenser's Serena and her predicament (Units 5–6, Section 7.10.1), in contrast, were both realistic and real. The emblemist's intention is a philosophical one, to give an *impression* of the function of Occasion. (The Italian word *impresa* meant an emblem or device with a motto, and was imported into English at about this time: such an emblem, when printed, was of course *impressed* on paper – a useful piece of etymological confusion, because it helps you with the almost dead metaphor of my word *impression*.) Study the picture and the poem now, making the connections between them, and establishing by the end of it the word which is the modern equivalent of Occasion.

2.6   **DISCUSSION**

The word you want is 'opportunity'. The interesting post-classical variants from Lycippus, the details of which are supplied by John Ferguson, are:

(i)   Occasion is feminine, whereas the Greek prototype was masculine, and a deity connected with athletics.

(ii)   The wheel in the picture is undoubtedly that of Fortune. That, and the fact that the wheel is horizontal instead of vertical, place the operation of Occasion within the sway of Fortune.

(iii)   The placing of the scene upon the sea may indicate some assimilation to Aphrodite, or the feeling of the illustrator that the wavering and unpredictable sea is the appropriate element for Occasion: there is no mention of the sea in the poem or in its classical model.

To sum up: this kind of artistic creation shows allegory operating as an esoteric interest in its own right rather than as a means of interpreting the universe. But it is the means, not the subject, that is esoteric: the subject, Occasion, was a real phenomenon of man's life, and hence a part of Nature which was generally understood to exist and to operate in the way the emblemist suggests.

The proper absorption of the emblematic tradition into the stream of English poetry of the period is best demonstrated by a brief quotation from Shakespeare's *Troilus and Cressida*, in which Ulysses is trying to persuade Achilles to rejoin the battle against the Trojans. The emblem he uses shows that Time gobbles up the memory of past good deeds, and the implication, which is made explicit later in the speech, is that Achilles must continually perform great deeds if he is to maintain his glory among the Greeks.

> Time hath, my lord, a wallet at his back,
> Wherein he puts alms for oblivion,
> A great-siz'd monster of ingratitudes.
> Those scraps are good deeds past, which are devour'd
> As fast as they are made, forgot as soon
> As done. Perseverance, dear my lord,
> Keeps honour bright.
>
> *Troilus and Cressida*, III.iii.145–51, in William Shakespeare,
> *The Complete Works*, ed. P. Alexander, Collins, 1951.

2.7   Now to the triumph. I take (Figure 4) a single pageant arch of the seven erected in London for *The Kings Entertainment in Passing to his Coronation* in 1604 (James I of England and VI of Scotland arrived in London from Edinburgh in May 1603, but an outbreak of the plague caused the festivities to be postponed until the following year). This pageant arch represents the city of London. It was designed by the architect Stephen Harrison, and the commentary and poetry were by Ben Jonson (*Ben Jonson*, ed. C. H. Herford, Percy and Evelyn Simpson, Oxford University Press, 1963, vol. VII, pp. 65–109). The top figure at the centre, under the word LONDINIVM, is Monarchia Britannica. She is flanked by the six daughters of the City's Genius; on her left by Gladness, Loving Affection and Unanimity, and on her right by Veneration, Promptitude and Vigilance. But it is the figure at her feet – though I'm well aware that you can't pick out the detail – as described by Jonson with which I want you to spend the moment or two we can spare on this subject. She is

THEOSOPHIA

or diuine *Wisedome*, all in white, a blue mantle seeded with starres, a crowne of starres on her head. Her garments figur'd truth, innocence, and cleerenesse. Shee was always looking vp; in her one hand shee sustayned a doue, in the other a serpent: the last to shew her subtiltie, the first her simplicitie; alluding to that text of Scripture, *Estote ergo prudentes sicut serpentes, & simplices sicut columbae* [be ye therefore wise as serpents, and harmless as doves – *Matthew* X, 16 – B.S.]. Her word

PER ME REGES REGNANT.
[By me kings reign – *Proverbs* VIII, 15 – B.S.]

Indicating, how by her, all kings doe gouerne, and that she is the foundation and strength of kingdomes, to which end, shee was here placed, vpon a cube, at the foot of the Monarchie, as her base and stay.

Herford and Simpson, op. cit., vol. VII, pp. 84–5.

Figure 4   The Londinium Arch at Fenchurch, from Stephen Harrison, Arches of Triumph, *1604 (The British Museum)*

2.8 It seems that King James did not wish to be wearied with tedious speeches. So the spoken proceedings were accordingly cut short, and the king may have missed at least some of the lesson the pageant arch was meant to teach him. This was unlike his predecessor, Queen Elizabeth, of one of whose early progresses through the City this story is told:

> At Cheapside there were two hills, each with a tree on it, one withered to represent a 'decayed commonweale', the other green to represent a 'flourishing commonweale', and between the two came forth Truth and Time. The point of this was not lost on Elizabeth who is said to have cried, 'And Time hath brought me hither!'
>
> Rosemary Freeman, op. cit., p. 49.

If Elizabeth had been with James in 1604, she would have noticed that Theosophia was securely sitting on a cube, not like the circus fairy Fortune, who was characteristically given a sphere to stand on, as Shakespeare's fine Welsh soldier, Fluellen, recognized in his remarks just before the battle of Agincourt:

> and she is painted also with a wheel, to signify to you, which is the moral of it, that she is turning, and inconstant, and mutability, and variation; and her foot, look you, is fixed upon a spherical stone, which rolls, and rolls, and rolls.
>
> Henry V III.vi.31–5 in William Shakespeare, *The Complete Works*, ed. P. Alexander, Collins, 1951.

2.9 The emblematic tradition's last important and independent manifestation in our period was in the Stuart Masque, a genre which was doomed socially and politically because the two kings its poets and designers served, James I and Charles I, presided over a system which was shortly to be discarded in the Civil War. It has survived in transmuted forms, absorbed into other genres, as my example from *Troilus and Cressida* indicates, and it was to have further life later in the new form of opera, which originated in Italy at the end of the sixteenth century, and came to England in the mid-seventeenth century. But that is another story.

Allardyce Nicoll (*Stuart Masques*, Harrap, 1938, p. 19) refers to the genre of the Stuart Masque as 'that rich and nobly foolish line of courtly entertainments which made magnificent the reigns of James and Charles'. That modern judgement receives unexpected confirmation from Ben Jonson himself, who fought 'Mr. Surveyor' (the architect and artist Inigo Jones, with whom he worked on court masques for twenty-six years) for the right to have his words considered as important as the visual symbolism: and losing the battle, pronounced the epitaph of the court masque as well as its best description, in his *An Expostulation with Inigo Jones* (1631):

> O Showes! Showes! Mighty Showes!
> The Eloquence of Masques! What need of prose
> Or Verse, or Sense t'express Immortall you?
> You are y^e [1] Spectacles of State! Tis true
> Court Hieroglyphicks! & all Artes affoord
> In ye mere perspectiue of an Inch board!
> Ye aske noe more then certeyne politique Eyes,
> Eyes y^t can pierce into ye Misteryes
> Of many Coulors! read them! & reuale
> Mythology there painted on slit deale!
> Oh, to make Boardes to speake! There is a taske!
> Painting & Carpentry are y^e soule of Masque.
>
> Herford and Simpson, op. cit., vol. VIII, pp. 403–4.

---

[1] A note by Catherine King on 'y-' as printed above. It derives from the way 'the' was written in the fifteenth and sixteenth centuries: ꝥe 1 = t, ꝥ = h, e = e. y was the nearest print letter to the shape ꝥ.

2.10   The emblematic tradition was part of the consciousness of all educated people, and must therefore be borne in mind when reading the poetry of the period, even though in its decline it spoke for a minority. We have come very far from the medieval tradition of allegory, which could be echoed by the Royalist poet Francis Quarles, as late as 1635:

> Before the knowledge of letters GOD was known by Hierogliphicks. And, indeed, what are the Heavens, the Earth, nay every Creature, but Hierogliphicks and Emblems of his Glory?
>
> Quoted by Rosemary Freeman, op. cit., p. 41.

2.11   The third reason why the habit of allegorizing lingered on in the poetry is more complex. It has to do with the entire way an artist, in this case a poet, saw himself in society. I shall attempt here only to indicate its salient features: if you want a full and informed presentation of the subject, Rosemond Tuve will give it you in her *Elizabethan and Metaphysical Imagery* (University of Chicago Press, Seventh impression, 1965). One of the most important chapters, that on *'Imitation' and Images*, is included in your recommended textbook of criticism (*Elizabethan Poetry: Modern Essays in Criticism*, ed. Paul J. Alpers, Oxford University Press, 1967, pp. 41–62), and I hope you manage to read it, fairly tough going though it is. For the moment, see how much of the poet's attitude to his role you can gather simply by reading one of the best known of Shakespeare's sonnets, 'Let me not to the marriage of true minds' (p. 235 of your set text). My guiding questions, which I limit for the time being, because we shall return to this poem later, are:

(i)   Do you perceive a personal experience behind the poem?

(ii)   If so, what is it, and how sure are you about it?

(iii)   What is the actual subject of the poem?

(iv)   What is the function of the imagery?

(v)   What are the sources of the imagery?

(vi)   To what extent, if any, is it a didactic poem?

2.12   **DISCUSSION**

I'm dodging the first two questions, because there is no objective evidence on which to base an answer. But the subject of the poem is the assertion that true love lasts until doom; the function of the imagery is to approve examples of permanence and scorn examples of impermanence; and the sources of the imagery are strictly traditional (mark, tempests, star, bark), even to the personification of Time with his sickle, and the tentative identification of Love as a young person with rosy lips and cheeks. Superficially, then, it is right to say that the mechanism and literal meaning of the poem are didactic. But we shall return to the poem later, and discover through working on it how a poetic convention in the hands of a major poet can seem virtually to disappear under a fusion of original thought and feeling. Rosemond Tuve does not mention this poem, but she does comment on the extraordinary frequency with which maxims of general conduct and belief occur in the love poetry of the age. And if they occur there, they will be still more frequent in other kinds of poetry, to which they appear, even to us of the twentieth century, more native.

Figure 5   The Triumph of Time over Fame: *sixteenth-century tapestry at Hampton Court Palace (Department of the Environment)*

2.13 Among the generally accepted beliefs upon which Shakespeare bases that poem is the very message that Elizabeth understood from those two mock trees on Cheapside, with their labels – that Truth is the Daughter of Time. So, if that poem is any guide, in Elizabethan poetry we must always be ready to find three characteristics:

(i) Imagery is likely to be used to exploit symbolic spiritual and moral values rather than to convey sensuous exactitude.

(ii) The general is likely to take precedence over the particular.

(iii) Personal experience is unlikely to be precisely described, although it is acknowledged as the occasion of poetry.

These characteristics are part of a broad general attitude found among poets. It is on the whole a public attitude, and in it I do not detect the kind of emphasis on individual expression which is characteristic of, say, Romantic poets of the late eighteenth and early nineteenth centuries, who were distinguished not only for their individualism as poets, but by their social and political awareness and reforming zeal. The thought of Elizabethan poets tended to represent new syntheses of existing social and moral ideas, and to be the harmonious product of people who broadly accepted the social and moral order of which they were members. But the poetic achievements of the Elizabethan age, as those of any other age, transcend any such general characteristics as may be discerned.

Figure 5 The Hampton Court Tapestry: The Triumph of Time over Fame (sixteenth century)
Commentary by Catherine King

This tapestry symbolizes the triumph of Time over Fame. Fame is usually symbolized as a winged girl who carries a trumpet to spread her fame, and is the centre of a triumphal procession of richly decked admirers. On this tapestry the bulk of the procession is in the left-hand section of the scene. Fame, labelled 'Renomee' and without her trumpet, is shown in the right-hand section, being driven swiftly away in the Chariot of Time – a figure who has the attributes of Cronos (Saturn) and Chronos (Time). This confusion (the addition of Saturn's grey beard and crutches to Time's wings) is described in a well-known essay by E. Panofsky in *Studies in Iconology* (Harper and Row, 1962).

The subject of a triumph was a favourite for household, 'furniture' decoration as it traditionally combined gay detail and the required 'moral' story. The subject is part of the Petrarchan tradition – Petrarch's poem *The Triumph of Eternity* describes the triumph of Chastity over Love; Death over Chastity; Fame over Death; Time over Fame and, finally, the triumph of Eternity over all human endeavour or memory. The serious strain in this allegory is played down in the tapestry but is present even in the symbols of the Zodiac – Gemini, Scorpio and Leo – which whirl over the heads of the figures, each pursued by, and pursuing, a couple of court ladies who are, perhaps, meant to represent the fleeting hours of Time.

3.0   MUTABILITY: *THE MUTABILITIE CANTOS,* BY EDMUND SPENSER

3.1   First, re-read my summary introductory statement about Mutability (1.2), and then study Figures 5 and 6, and the commentary on them by Catherine King.

3.2   Spenser, 'the master of everybody' among Elizabethan poets, as T. S. Eliot calls him in his essay on Sir John Davies (Alpers, p. 325), naturally has the most philosophical and poetic things to say about Mutability, and I begin this section with a brief indication of the subject of what are called *The Mutabilitie Cantos*. These were first printed in the 1609 Folio of *The Faerie Queene*, under the following title: *Two Cantos of Mutabilitie: Which, both for Forme and Matter, appeare to be parcell of some following Booke of the FAERIE QUEENE, Under the Legend of Constancie. Never before imprinted.* But since there is no reference in the cantos which might link them to *The Faerie Queene*, and they appear to make up a complete work, even to the extent of concluding with a prayer which sums up Spenser's attitude to the subject matter, it is usual for the 116 stanzas to be considered as a separate poem, whether they are regarded as having been originally designed to be included in *The Faerie Queene* or not.

3.3   The poem presents the attempt of Mutability, characterized as a Titaness in rebellion against Jove, to obtain rule over the universe. She first challenges the moon in her palace, thus darkening the world. When the inhabitants of heaven appeal to Jove, but before the latter can take action against her, she goes to Jove's high palace to plead her case. He judges against her, but she appeals to the God of Nature, and Jove determines that the case be heard at Arlo-hill in Ireland. The last twenty stanzas of the first canto (Canto VI of the seventh book of *The Faerie Queene*, which is its conventional designation, following Matthew Lownes, the printer of the 1609 Folio) are a digression, in which Spenser describes the country around Kilcolman, where he began to live in 1589, and accounts for its desolateness with a tale of Diana and Faunus. The second canto mainly comprises Mutability's claim to sovereignty: before the assembled gods, mortals and creatures, she claims to dominate with her principle of Change all the attributes of earth and nature – living creatures human and brute, the four elements, the seasons, the months, day and night, and finally life and death. In his reply, Jove points out that all change is subject to Time, which is ruled by the gods, who are therefore superior. Mutability's final claim is that the gods themselves, and even the heavens with their changeable motions, are subject to her. The poem concludes with Nature's confirmation of Jove's argument, and her prophecy of an end to even the limited domination of Mutability. The poet's final prayer links that prophecy with the triumph of religion. Spenser's summary of the argument, which appears in two quatrains, one at the head of each canto, is:

> Proud Change (not pleasd, in mortall things,
>   beneath the Moone, to raigne)
> Pretends, as well of Gods, as Men,
>   to be the Soueraine.
>
> Pealing, from Joue, to Natur's Bar,
>   bold Alteration pleades
> Large evidence: but Nature soone
>   her righteous Doome areads.

This, and all following quotations from *The Mutabilitie Cantos*, are from *The Poetical Works of Edmund Spenser*, ed. J. C. Smith and E. de Selincourt, Oxford University Press, 1912.

3.4   The first of these two quatrains needs some explanation. 'Mortal things' exist 'beneath the Moone', immortal things above it. In the sub-lunary region, which is Earth and its atmosphere, matter is composed of the four elements – fire, air, earth and water. When these are imperfectly mixed, as they are generally agreed to be, matter is subject to decay and disorder; but they yearn for perfect separation, which will give them rest instead of the immutable mutability they are undergoing. Above the moon was the fifth element, or quintessence, ether, of which heavenly or *ethereal* bodies are composed. Ether is latent in sub-lunary things. As with the elements, so with movement: perfection above the moon, imperfection but latent perfection below. 'Beneath the Moone' movement can happen in any direction, but above it is always circular – a condition which gives what Spenser calls in his last stanza 'stedfast rest', that is, paradoxically, mutable immutability. Copernicus, as you will remember, was partly prompted to one of his discoveries by belief in that circular movement. The Aristotelian and Ptolemaic system he helped to supplant was partly based on an attempt to show that, although heavenly bodies did 'move' and 'alter' – that they did not invariably conform to the ideal of circular movement had been observed – they were not as 'corrupt' or 'changed' as sub-lunary objects.

Here are some short extracts from the poem, on each of which there is an exercise. The *Discussion and Suggested Answers* begin at 3.9. When you have done this work, I hope you will be able to read other poems in this group with better enjoyment and understanding.

1   (From Spenser's own description of Mutability at the beginning of the poem – Canto VI, part of stanza 1, and stanza 6):

> What man that sees the euer-whirling wheele
>   Of *Change*, the which all mortall things doth sway,
>   But that therby doth find, and plainly feele,
>   How MVTABILITIE in them doth play
>   Her cruell sports, to many mens decay?
>   . . .
> Ne shee the lawes of Nature onely brake,
>   But eke of Iustice, and of Policie;
>   And wrong of right, and bad of good did make,
>   And death for life exchanged foolishlie:
>   Since which, all liuing wights haue learn'd to die,
>   And all this world is woxen daily worse.
>   O pittious worke of MVTABILITIE!
>   By which, we all are subject to that curse,
> And death in stead of life haue sucked from our Nurse.

(a)   What does Mutability actually *do*? Does her function strike any biblical, or possibly classical, echo in your mind?

(b)   Who is 'our Nurse'?

3.5   2   And now to Spenser's view of Nature, at least as far as Nature is portrayed in the poem. In Canto VI, when Jove tells her to cease her 'idle claim', Mutability appeals in these terms (stanza 35, first six lines):

> But thee, O Ioue, no equall Iudge I deeme
>   Of my desert, or of my dewfull Right;
>   That in thine owne behalfe maist partiall seeme:
>   But to the highest him, that is behight
>   Father of Gods and men by equall might;
>   To weet, the God of Nature, I appeale.

3.6   Upon arriving at the great gathering on Arlo-hill, Nature is described thus (Canto VII, stanzas 5–6):

> Then forth issewed (great goddesse) great dame *Nature*,
>   With goodly port and gracious Majesty;
>   Being far greater and more tall of stature
>   Then any of the gods or Powers on hie:
>   Yet certes by her face and physnomy,
>   Whether she man or woman inly were,
>   That could not any creature well descry:
>   For, with a veile that wimpled euery where,
> Her head and face was hid, that mote to none appeare.

> That some doe say was so by skill deuized,
>   To hide the terror of her vncouth hew,
>   From mortall eyes that should be sore agrized;
>   For that her face did like a Lion shew,
>   That eye of wight could not indure to view:
>   But others tell that it so beautious was,
>   And round about such beames of splendor threw,
>   That it the Sunne a thousand times did pass,
> Ne could be seene, but like an image in a glass.

Applying to this description of Nature the methods of allegorical interpretation you studied in Units 5–6, what do you learn about her (him)?

3.7   3   Unfortunately, I cannot ask you to spend time on either the further description of Nature and the joy she arouses at the gathering (stanzas 7–13), or the procession of allegorized attributes of earth presented by Mutability in support of her argument (stanzas 28–46). But here is the core of Mutability's argument that the heavens, and Nature herself, are subject to her (stanza 55):

> Besides, the sundry motions of your Spheares,
>   So sundry waies and fashions as clerkes faine,
>   Some in short space, and some in longer yeares;
>   What is the same but alteration plaine?
>   Onely the starrie skie doth still remaine:
>   Yet do the Starres and Signes therein still moue,
>   And euen it self is mov'd, as wizards saine.
>   But all that moueth, doth mutation loue:
> Therefore both you and them to me I subiect proue.

(a)   Where else in this course have you met these ideas about the movement of heavenly bodies?

(b)   Mutability is referred to as *Change* in the second line of Canto VI. What other words in the above stanza are used by Spenser as near-synonyms for Mutability?

3.8   4   And now for Nature's judgement in the case of Mutability *v.* Jove (stanzas 58–9):

> I well consider all that ye haue sayd,
>> And find that all things stedfastnes doe hate
>> And changed be: yet being rightly wayd
>> They are not changed from their first estate;
>> But by their change their being doe dilate;
>> And turning to themselues at length againe,
>> Doe worke their owne perfection so by fate:
>> Then ouer them Change doth not rule and raigne;
> But they raigne ouer change, and doe their states maintaine.
>
> Cease therefore daughter further to aspire,
>> And thee content thus to be rul'd by me:
>> For thy decay thou seekst by thy desire;
>> But time shall come that all shall changed bee,
>> And from thenceforth, none no more change shall see.
>> So was the *Titaness* put down and whist,[1]
>> And Ioue confirm'd in his imperiall see,
>> Then was that whole assembly quite dismisst,
> And *Natur's* self did vanish, whither no man wist.

[1] silenced

Stanza 58 contains the core of apparently paradoxical thought which is the basis of the whole poem. To satisfy yourself that you know what it means, paraphrase it. Or, if you think your paraphrase might run to the length of a minor assignment, write a gloss on the parts you need to ponder before they yield good sense.

DISCUSSION AND SUGGESTED ANSWERS

3.9   1   (a)   The role of Mutability is surprisingly like that of the serpent in Genesis 3, in that she made human beings subject to death. Breaking the laws of Nature, Justice and Policy is an activity appropriate to the Devil of the Judaeo-Christian system and the banished Titans of classical mythology, all of whom were descended, through their mother Gaea, the personification of the Earth, from Chaos. (Chaos, by the way, in classical mythology, was the formless void, the Abyss or Chasm: it is interesting that our figurative use of it to describe utter confusion and disorder first appears in our language just after Spenser's death.)

1   (b)   'our Nurse' is Nature.

3.10   2   Mutability's appeal to Nature subsists on two assumptions – Nature is 'Father of Gods and men by equall might', and is, by implication, an 'equall (i.e. fair) Iudge'. As an allegorical figure, her size represents her superiority, her 'goodly port' the high morality inherent in sound order. That her sex is indeterminate represents the completeness with which, as an anthropomorphic figure, she subsumes all living creation: Nature could not be presented, limited, as a mere god or goddess. But the English language lacks a singular personal pronoun applicable to both sexes, and so Nature, having first been called 'the God' (in stanza 35), settles down in the poem as 'she'. The wimple is the veil of mystery, hiding the terror and the beauty of Nature, which are both majestic, the one lion-like and the other sun-like. 'Some doe say' and 'But others tell' remove the appearance as described from the realm of ascertained fact; Spenser assumes that human sight can bear neither Nature's face of terror nor her face of beauty, and that is his way of indicating the superhuman and inscrutable power which controls the universe.

3.11   That interpretation of the allegory was straightforward but the answer, viewed as a coherent group of beliefs about Nature, is unsatisfactory. This is because the Renaissance conception of Nature is complex, diverse in origin, and even paradoxical; while, considered as a goddess, her relation to the other gods and to fate is ambiguous. Generally speaking, both the gods and fate are aspects of nature, and therefore subject to Nature. But theologically speaking, nature was not only the whole of creation visible and invisible, but was thought of as something like a principle of order in the mind of God, upon which the existence of the universe was believed to be based. 'Naturally'(!) in formal Christian theology, Nature as a separate force had no existence of any kind. Part of E. M. W. Tillyard's summary of the views of Richard Hooker (in *Of the Laws of Ecclesiastical Politie*, 1594, the great Elizabethan defence of the Anglican position) on Nature is relevant here.

> She cannot be allowed a will of her own or the rank of a kind of goddess. She is not even an agent with her eye ever fixed on God's principles; rather she is the direct and involuntary tool of God himself. The different phenomena of nature *must* perform their own proper functions in order to retain their identities, but they are not conscious of this. They work not on nature's initiative but on God's, by the pressure of his Providence.
>
> *The Elizabethan World Picture*, Peregrine Books, 1963, p. 61.

Spenser follows Hooker in the position reached at the end of the poem. You will find these ideas about Nature useful when you study *King Lear*, and will find Hooker's and Spenser's bases good starting points from which to tackle Shakespeare's conception of Nature in that play. The essay by A. S. P. Woodhouse, 'Nature and Grace in the Faerie Queene', which is in your recommended critical support text (Alpers, pp. 345–79) is useful for study of much of the literature in Units 29–34.

3.12   3 (a)   You surely remember most of this from your study of Copernicus, when you examined it as a precise system. Spenser is using the system metaphorically, as a poet, and that should be your interest rather than checking his accuracy. For example, Mutability's 'But all that moueth, doth mutation loue' is inaccurate: in the cosmos objects are dissatisfied until they find eternal rest. Mutability is advancing a Heraclitan argument. It is only when the movement is perfect that 'all doth love mutation'. Try to remember that when you come to the theme of music in Elizabethan poetry. 'Alteration' of the spheres took place according to both the Ptolemaic and Copernican systems, but 'Yet do the Starres and Signes therein still moue' assures us that Spenser is thinking in strictly Ptolemaic terms.

3 (b)   Mutation; Alteration (which you have already met in the Shakespeare sonnet you looked at when reading the Introduction). So, whenever you meet Mutability, Mutation, Change or Alteration in Elizabethan poetry, resist thinking of them in simple terms: almost always, the poet is referring to a fairly complex concept which has an essential place in the religious and moral philosophy of the time – a dynamic principle operating, as you will see (4 and 3.14 below) sometimes in opposition to Constancy, and sometimes as part of the mechanism by which Constancy subsists.

3.13   4   The judgement given by Nature is fundamentally in harmony with religious precept. The change inherent in growth and development – 'all things . . . by their change their being do dilate' – is part of a system which is itself constant. By the maintenance of this system, 'all things . . . do worke their owne perfection so by fate'; and Nature goes on to imply that what Mutability is seeking by her claim to supplant the permanent powers (chiefly gods, goddesses and Nature) is a situation in which her own power will weaken. It will weaken because the system which allows her power to operate on the whole beneficially will have disappeared. All that is implied in the line:

> For thy decay thou seekst by thy desire.

One problem remains, the two-word qualification which most Elizabethans would have accepted, but which nevertheless, to them as to thinkers of all other ages, poses a question which must be asked whenever the meaning of existence is pondered: 'by fate'. I referred above to change operating under a constant system by 'growth and development': if I had also written 'by event' (which must include, for example, war, famine, pestilence, accident), I would have added the element of disorder inherent in the principle of change. Nature barely tips her cap to such a notion with her 'by fate'.

In stanza 59 Nature looks forward to the time when creation will reach a state of static perfection – the Golden Age, the Millennium, the new heaven and the new earth of Revelation, or whatever – by the finally transforming act of change:

> But time shall come that all shall changed be.

Notice, by the way, that Nature is the only person present on Arlo-hill about whose departure Spenser is specific:

> And Natur's self did vanish, whither no man wist.

This mystery rounds off and completes his allegory of her.

3.14   I now come to the paradoxical but beautifully balanced conclusion to the poem, the last two stanzas, which bring the whole thought of the poem into the personal focus of Spenser's own belief about the world, and his faith. The debate in the poem between Mutability and her opponents raised a number of widely held beliefs about the principle of change: the brilliance and persistence of the threat posed by Mutability symbolized the attractions and the dangers Renaissance intellectuals felt she represented, and the concluding judgement of Nature both justified the system of order upon which the universe was based and explained why religious faith remained possible in face of Mutability's harmful activities. I say the ending is personal because Spenser's ending expresses in one stanza his horror and concern at the extent of Mutability's depredations, and in the other his yearning for the arrival of heaven on earth. It is the first of these two stanzas which I should like you to bear in mind as you read and think about the other poems in this section, because it is so characteristic; and now that you have placed its beliefs within a system of thought, you will be able to recognize and place the theme whenever it crops up in poetry, remembering always that the poets' use of that system was generally metaphysical and would have satisfied neither an exact scientist nor a strict theologian of the day. For your satisfaction at this moment, however, I hope you will read both stanzas with equal emphasis. I called the ending paradoxical, because one part of it, concentrating on the evil power of Mutability, emphasizes afresh her essential force in the desires of living beings:

But all that moueth, doth mutation loue:	(see 3.7 above: Mutability's words)
. . . all things stedfastnes doe hate	
And changed be:	(see 3.8 above: Nature's words)
In all things else she bears the greatest sway.	(Spenser's ending)
For, all that moueth, doth in *Change* delight:	(Spenser's ending)

49

while the other looks forward to a time of eternal rest when no more change can happen. It is a paradox deeply built into every religious system which offers the hope of heaven, and it is dignified by the drive of thinking and moral man towards perfection and permanence.

Another view of the ending is possible: that since Spenser presents the dominion of Mutability on earth, and the rule of God in heaven, as strictly consecutive, his almost continuous celebration of movement throughout the poem must be regarded as superseded, so that 'paradoxical' is a false description of the ending. A Christian might argue that 'heaven' can be dynamically conceived; but Spenser does not write of that, unless stanza 58 (see 3.8 again), from 'yet being rightly wayd' to the end, be regarded as a description of the process of heaven.

Dwell on the two stanzas a little, reading them aloud if possible. The slow pace, the judicious debating qualifiers ('yet', 'me seemes', 'For', 'But') mute the passion into detachment without muffling it, and so provide an ideal basis for the one-line prayer which ends the poem.

3.15   The VIII Canto, 'vnperfite' (as Lownes labelled it):

1

When I bethinke me on that speech whyleare,
  Of *Mutability*, and well it way:
  Me seemes, that though she all vnworthy were
  Of the Heav'ns Rule; yet very sooth to say,
  In all things else she beares the greatest sway.
  Which makes me loath this state of life so tickle,
  And loue of things so vaine to cast away;
  Whose flowering pride, so fading and so fickle,
Short *Time* shall soone cut down with his consuming sickle.

2

Then gin I thinke on that which Nature sayd,
  Of that same time when no more *Change* shall be,
  But stedfast rest of all things firmely stayd
  Vpon the pillours of Eternity,
  That is contrayr to *Mutabilitie*:
  For, all that moueth, doth in *Change* delight:
  But thence-forth all shall rest eternally
  With Him that is the God of Sabbaoth hight:
O that great Sabbaoth God, graunt me that Saboaths sight.

4.0 FURTHER POEMS ON MUTABILITY: DEATH, TIME AND MELANCHOLY

4.1   Perhaps, in my attempt to help you to a quite new frame of mind, I have been guilty of too much initial generalizing about Elizabethan poetry. So please turn now to a poem which, though in subject it fits the present theme, has characteristics, both in poetic diction and thought, for which you have not been prepared. It is Samuel Daniel's *Ulysses and the Siren* (p. 81 of your set text). The basis of this debate poem is in the twelfth book of the *Odyssey*, which tells how Odysseus (Ulysses, the Latin form of the name, is more common in English literature) and his companions, seeking their homeland, Ithaca, pass the island of the Sirens, mythical monsters, half-woman and half-bird, who so charm seamen with their ravishing song that they forget everything and die of hunger.

In the *Odyssey*, the hero plugs his sailors' ears with wax so that they may row past without hearing, but listens himself, bound to the mast so that he cannot respond to the alluring song. Daniel's protagonists debate the values which cluster symbolically round their action in the ancient Greek poem, values which were deeply interesting to the age of humanism. Read the poem, making notes on

(i)   the successive subjects of the debate, and their interrelation

(ii)   the poetic diction

(iii)   the tone.

4.2   **DISCUSSION**

(i)   The fundamental subject is the opposition of the life of ease and pleasure to the life of heroic endeavour. The former, though it begins with a basely sensual proposition in the first stanza, takes its strength from more noble aspects of the passive life, such as pacifism and loving kindness, and tilts quite effectively at such sacred cows of the aristocratic life of action as honour and fame. But it is the life of heroic endeavour as represented by Ulysses which naturally and conventionally triumphs, though not so easily that the arguments of the other side are forgotten. We tend to forget that the Christian humanists of the Renaissance could and did condemn war-making, even in the presence of belligerent kings. For example, when Henry VIII was preparing for war against the French, Colet in his Good Friday sermon before the king 'praised the victory of Christ as the only victory worth winning; he pointed out the difficulty of Christian conduct in time of war, and spoke much to discourage the intending soldiers'. (G. K. Hunter, *Humanism and Courtship* in Alpers, p. 26.) The ending of the poem is surprising, in a way. Beauty (for of course Sirens, with their fatal power to attract, were bound to be considered beautiful), behaving – at least I think so – as a true daughter of Mutability, makes a dynamic sacrifice of herself to bring the conflict in the poem to a state of resolution. Yet discussion of the nature of beauty is extrusive: perhaps Daniel grasped at it as the means to conclude the debate, rightly feeling that there can be no resolution between the total opposites of the passive life and the active life.

(ii)   What! No allegory, no imagery except an occasional dead metaphor (such as the begetting of honour in the third stanza)? A spare vocabulary of exact meaning, with few superfluous adjectives, and those are conventional; a scrupulous attention to natural word order in spite of the exigencies of a metre characterized by short lines and an unvarying rhyme scheme; repeated concentrations of epigrammatic force, which read as with the ease of good prose. All is what we should expect of a man whose main contribution to the late Elizabethan debate about the art of poetry was to oppose the automatic application of 'all the Rules of idle Rhetorique'. C. S. Lewis (*English Literature in the Sixteenth Century Excluding Drama*, Oxford University Press, 1954, p. 530) notes Daniel's 'masculine and unstrained majesty' when he is at his best, and compares him with Wordsworth for his severity of approach and his power to think in verse.

(iii) The tone is philosophic, judicious, urbane. Serious views on serious subjects are brought to exact focus in nicely balanced juxtaposition. All that is lacking – supposing one were entitled to demand more than Daniel gives us –

is a sense of involvement, on the part of either the protagonists or the poet, a difference of diction to distinguish the two characters, and a creatively original thought.

4.3 Now for four poems on the subject of death, each of which has a different approach and form, though all are related to our theme of Mutability, Death being the means of ending 'this state of life so tickle', and the chief and most dreaded of Time's punctuation marks. The four poems are Shakespeare's *Dirge for Fidele* (p. 230), Raleigh's sonnet *To his son* (p. 217), Southwell's *Upon the image of Death* (p. 246), and Nashe's song: *Adieu, farewell earth's bliss* (p. 198). Read them and make notes on

(i) subject

(ii) mood or tone

(iii) style or presentation.

Sometimes you may find that the form of the poem invites you to deal with these separately, sometimes together.

4.4 **DISCUSSION**

Dirge for Fidele

(i) In *Cymbeline*, Fidele is the name taken by the heroine Imogen, when she disguises herself as a boy to avoid those who would kill her; and she is not dead, but under the influence of one of those drugs so convenient to the Elizabethan dramatists, which give the appearance of death.

(ii) Since the audience know this, the beautiful dirge, with its gentle melancholy and reconciliation with the fact of death, is distanced into a mood of reflection and general pathos, in which great medieval themes, such as the levelling power of death (especially in the last couplets of the first three stanzas) and contempt of the turbulence of this world (in the second and third stanzas), have their place. The last stanza is a charm to prevent malignant supernatural power disturbing the eternal rest of the dead Fidele. You may know Shakespeare's own epitaph:

> Good friend, for Jesu's sake forbear
> To dig the dust enclosed here.
> Blest be the man that spares these stones,
> And curst be he that moves my bones.

(iii) Have a look at the form of the first three stanzas. The standard metre of the first four lines of each stanza is trochaic, and of the concluding couplet iambic (except for the first line of the first concluding couplet, which is trochaic); every line contains four feet, but of the trochaic lines, only the second and fourth of the first stanza are complete, the feminine endings of 'rages' and 'wages' providing this exceptional regularity. The generally trochaic structure, the preponderance of long syllables, and the pauses enforced by the uncompleted trochees, give the poem a slow, measured beat appropriate to the subject.

The first four lines of each stanza propose a course of action and an argument of solace, in the form of a repeated imperative ('Fear no more . . .' etc.) followed by a statement (this process is doubled in the second stanza); and then follows the couplet which, though it varies from stanza to stanza, is recognizably a refrain. Note how these refrains refer to Fidele with increasing emphasis. The first is quite general, referring to all golden (i.e. beautiful and, just possibly, though it could not refer to Fidele, rich) young people; in the second the supposed corpse becomes 'this', and in the last it is 'thee'. This progression gives structure to the threnody, which comes to a climax with the mysterious and lovely charm. Indeed, 'Quiet consummation have'. Remember that the dirge is for acting as well as singing: the mechanics of interment and invocation can never be ignored when a dirge is being considered or performed.

4.5 *To his son*

(i)   There is a special pathos in a poem about execution written in a gay–grim mood by a poet who was himself executed, and Raleigh spent many years of his life in daily expectation of losing his head. The central subject is a prayer that his son will not be hanged, for Mutability, come what may, *will* assure that there is a 'meeting day' of 'the wood, the weed, the wag'. Let someone else be hanged then.

(ii)   I find that this superb poem, in its reliance on a folk theme – the wood, the weed and the wag – its absence of decoration and its unblinking reliance on strong, monosyllabic verbs, with no adjectives at all except those attached to the vocative ('pretty knave', 'dear child'), is medieval and pre-Drab in spirit. It has marked affinities with the poetry of sin and death of an earlier age: the English poetry of that kind is mostly anonymous, but you may have met the work of the French poet Villon, in which a Renaissance revolt against the grand apparatus by which humans suffer and die was beginning to be expressed.

(iii)   Raleigh rebelled against the grand apparatus partly because, as you have read, he felt rejected by one of its main functionaries, the Court. He challenges the set-up subtly in this poem: his grim description of the state of things is presented almost playfully as a lesson to a child, which concludes with the distinctly ironical mixed instruction to 'bless thee, and *beware*, and let us pray'. No unqualified trust in the powers above to protect the young.

4.6 *Upon the image of Death*

(i)   To pass from Raleigh to Southwell is to go yet deeper into the medieval spirit of thinking and feeling. The subject, its treatment, and all the details in this poem, especially the references to the skull (stanza 2) and the Biblical and Greek and Roman heroes, had been commonplaces of poetry, prose, romance and sermon for three hundred years. And that's where the interest lies, in a poem published in 1595, when most of Shakespeare's sonnets had been written and much of Donne's secular poetry was in circulation in manuscript. For Southwell was an English Catholic, who had left England young to obtain a Catholic upbringing, had become an ardent Jesuit, and was sent back to England to do mission work for the Society of Jesus. His role was so important that discovery, arrest and martyrdom (the accounts of his torture and death are grisly and pathetic in the extreme) were virtually automatic consequences. All his writing, whether in prose or poetry, was didactic and designed to serve his cause. So this poem must be thought of as aimed at a popular audience. It was published in a collection of devotional poetry put together in 1595 by Catholic editors, who 'were careful to select poems that did not express specifically Catholic doctrine' (*The Poems of Robert Southwell S.J.*, ed. McDonald and Brown, Oxford University Press, 1967, p. lvi) because they were concerned

to obtain a good circulation for the book, to avoid giving flagrant offence, and to avoid being prosecuted for publishing a popish book.

(ii)   So it is as popular, public poetry that we should look at what might appear at first sight to be a private poem of meditation. Looked at in this light, the well-tried teaching technique of applying traditional cultural and religious matter to personal experience (at least two 'I's in every stanza but the penultimate), and the implicit exhortation to the reader to avoid sin in order to die well, make perfect sense and decorum.

(iii) Poor Southwell had virtually to re-learn his native English after years in exile of using Latin and Italian daily; his occasional awkwardness and lack of fluency – and you may find your own examples in this poem – are attributable to that rather than to a deliberate preference for antique language, or to any of the language problems which bothered earlier Elizabethans whom Cicely Havely has discussed. But his power over the poetic form he uses (did you spot it as the same stanza form as the *Dirge of Fidele*, though the metre is iambic and not trochaic?), and his use of the variable refrain to achieve progression and climax, are fine.

4.7   *Song: Adieu, farewell earth's bliss*

(i)   I deliberately put Nashe's marvellous poem at the end of this group, because I wanted you to enjoy it (afresh, perhaps, because it is in all the anthologies, and you may have met it) after absorbing the background which the other three poems incidentally provide for it. The single new feature in subject matter is the placing of the whole matter of Death within the context of the plague, which repeatedly visited London during these years.

(ii) and (iii)   There is a magnificent engagement with the processes of Mutability; decay and vicissitude are positively celebrated with a rich feeling for the beauty and heroism of their victims (stanzas 3 and 4) – a defiance which reaches its logical climax with the last line before the final refrain:

> Mount we unto the sky.

Only the refrain – and note how it is always introduced by the warning rhyme in the previous line – remains on the conventional liturgical level. If we had the music – for again, this is a *song*, from Nashe's single surviving comedy – it would be interesting to see how it reflected the change in each stanza for the refrain, and the splendid modulation into the triumphant mood of the last stanza.

4.8   And now for four poems on the theme of Time, two for quick reading first, and then two for more detailed consideration. Dekker's Prologue from *The Whore of Babylon* (p. 97) has a fresh glow of imagination about it; I ask you to read it for three reasons:

(i)   it is yet another example of theatre being related to the great business of general life and thought,

(ii)   I wanted you to read at least one popular meditation on the theme of Time, and this is what it is, though it is the prologue to a play, and

(iii)   it shows implicitly that even a theatre audience was expected to know what Elizabeth perceived in the anecdote I quoted in Section 2.8, and Shakespeare based many sonnets on – that Truth is the daughter of Time.

The other poem to which I want you to give brief attention is Middleton's *The Golden Age* (p. 197), in which the poet turns a standard thought about the steady decline of humanity upon a standard grouse of Elizabethan poets –

that their literary efforts were not well enough rewarded. Marlowe included the same thought in the conclusion to the first Sestiad of *Hero and Leander*:

> And to this day is every scholar poor,
> Gross gold from them runs headlong to the boor.

The Fates, he writes

>   have concluded
> That Midas' brood shall sit in Honour's chair,
> To which the Muses' sons are only heir:
> And fruitful wits, that inaspiring are,
> Shall discontent run into regions far.
>
>   *Marlowe's Poems*, ed. L. C. Martin, Methuen, 1931, p. 51, lines 471–2, 473–7.

It was indeed an age when intelligent men of independent mind found it hard to earn a congenial living unless they consented to be dependents of nobility. Now read the Dekker and Middleton poems.

4.9   The two finer poems for which Time supplies a theme are Peele's *A sonnet* (p. 203) and Raleigh's *Nature that washed her hands in milk* (p. 213). First, read the note on *Polyhymnia* on page 281: then, on your first reading of *A sonnet*, note the subject elements of which the poem is composed. In the following discussion, I shall provide further background information, and then ask you to read the poem again.

4.10   Before I discuss the poem, I should like you to listen to the musical setting of it on the accompanying gramophone record. It is by John Dowland (1563–1626).

DISCUSSION

In the first stanza we have the familiar commonplaces about youth and age, and time, and an unobtrusive and fundamentally religious statement about Constancy (the three abstract nouns in the last line) and the Mutability of this world's pleasures and attributes (penultimate line). The second stanza is all symbolic picture and action appropriate to the retiring warrior; you might say that the helmet as a beehive is an esoteric emblem. The third stanza leaves the world of action firmly behind, and links the religious emphasis with a compliment to Queen Elizabeth and a protestation of loyalty in the knight's new role of beadsman (don't fail to look up this word if you're not quite sure of the meaning).

I want you now to read – however skimmingly you wish – a few paragraphs about *Polyhymnia*, because you will see from them how formal devices which we connect with Elizabethan art and poetry were part of real life, at least for the hero of this piece. Polyhymnia is a work

> Describing, The honourable Triumph at Tylt, before her
> Maiestie . . . With Sir Henrie Lea, his resignation of
> honour at Tylt, to her Maiestie, and receiued by the
> right honorable, the Earle of Cumberland.
>
>   *The Works of George Peele*, ed. A. H. Bullen 1888, reissued by the
>   Kennikat Press, Inc., 1966, Vol. II, p. 281.

Sir Henry Lea had instituted the performance of a triumph on every anniversary of Elizabeth's succession, and this one, in the Tiltyard at Westminster in 1590, was the occasion of his retiring and handing over his duties as Queen's Champion to the Earl of Cumberland. Bullen prefaces the text of *Polyhymnia* with a contemporary description of the event:

> Her maiestie, beholding these armed knights (i.e. Sir Henry Lea and the Earl of Cumberland) coming towards her, did suddenly heare a musicke so sweete and secret, as euery one thereat greatly marueiled. And hearkening to that excellent melodie, the earth, as it were, opening, there appeared a Pauilion, made of white taffata, containing eight score elles, being in proportion like vnto the sacred Temple of the Virgins Vestall ... upon the altar also were layd certaine princely presents, which after by three virgins were presented vnto her maiestie.
>
> Bullen, op. cit., p. 282.

On a crowned pillar hung a prayer for the Queen, worked in letters of gold. The singing of *A Sonnet* to 'the musicke aforesayd' was the first event of the proceedings. During the triumph, Sir Henry Lea

> offered vp his armour at the foot of her maiesties Crowned Pillar; and kneeling vpon his knees, presented the Earle of Cumberland, humbly beseeching she would be pleased to accept him for her knight ... Her majesty gratiously accepting of that offer, this aged knight armed the earle, and mounted him vpon his horse. That being done, he put vpon his owne person a side coat of blacke veluet pointed vnder the arme, and couered his head (in lieu of an helmet) with a buttoned cap of the countrey fashion. After all these ceremonies, for diuers dayes hee ware vpon his cloake a crowne embrodered, with a certaine motto or deuice, but what his intention therein was, himselfe best knoweth.
>
> Bullen, op. cit., p. 284.

Look at the poem again, and see how it gains from being placed, and how it might gain still more if written in the first person, as it was printed in 1602 in Segar's *Honor, Military and Ciuill*.

> My saint is sure of mine vnspotted hart
>
> Bullen, op. cit., p. 283.

becomes much more definitely a protestation of feudal loyalty than of virtuous faith and conduct, 'my saint' being, of course, Queen Elizabeth. The whole event of which the poem forms a part, showing Sir Henry Lea living his own symbolism with the help of a poet, has quite a different flavour from that of one of the late court masques of which it is a forbear.

4.11   Again, I place last in a group of poems the one on which I want you to spend most time, and on which I propose to write least. But like many poems ascribed to Raleigh, this one presents problems. When love is mentioned in a Raleigh poem, one expects it to have some connection with Queen Elizabeth; but Agnes Latham is surely right when she comments:

> Here we are dealing with a poem Raleigh could not have meant for the Queen. The descriptions are too sensuous, and the theme of time destroying love and beauty would have been far from congenial. It is not really a love poem at all, but a lament for the inevitable passing of life and joy.
>
> *Sir Walter Raleigh: Selected Prose and Poetry*, Athlone Press, 1965, pp. 212–13.

That comment should help you to view the personifications in the poem correctly, though I think you may have some slight difficulty on your first reading as I did, in correctly allocating all the pronouns and relatives: Love and Time are masculine throughout, Nature feminine. In the third stanza, the 'her' in the fifth line refers to the mistress Nature has created for Love, and the 'her' in the last line to Nature. Also, note that the first line of the fourth stanza means 'But Time which doth despise Nature'. For the rest, the controlled violence, whether the preoccupation is with the sensual female body or the despairs of Mutability, and the very fine economy in the use of adjectives, should imprint characteristic Raleigh on your mind. No wonder that Raleigh remembered the last stanza, and adapted it the night before being beheaded.

> These Verses following were made by Sir Walter Raleigh the night before he died and left at the Gate House.
> Even such is Time which takes in trust
> Our youth, our joys, and all we have,
> And pays us but with age and dust;
> Who in the dark and silent grave
> When we have wandered all our ways
> Shuts up the story of our days.
>   And from which earth and grave and dust
>   The Lord shall raise me up I trust.
>
> Latham, op. cit., p. 59.

Read it carefully, and listen to the reading on the accompanying gramophone record.

4.12   To end the theme treatment of Mutability, here are four poems, three of which express pathos and disillusion, and reflect melancholy aspects of man's confrontation with life, while the fourth disdains the relief of lamentation, and poses a Stoic riposte to conventional pessimism. They are:

Sir Francis Bacon's	*The world's a bubble*	(p. 36)
Samuel Daniel's sonnet	*Care-charmer sleep*	(p. 78)
John Marston's	*Prologue from Antonio's Revenge*	(p. 191)
Ben Jonson's	*To the world, a farewell for a gentle-*	(p. 161)
	woman, virtuous and noble	

4.13   First, a word about Melancholy. The word means 'Black bile', which in ancient physiology was thought to be one of the four humours, the others being phelgm, blood and choler. A just balance among these four made up a 'good humour', and if one of them was dominant, the result was an 'ill humour'. You'll meet the humours again when you study English Renaissance drama. The simplest way to get an idea of the huge range of the subject, as it applied to Elizabethans and Jacobeans, is to visit your local library, take from the shelf any modern edition of the three volumes of Robert Burton's *The Anatomy of Melancholy* (1621), and briefly scan the Synopses of the First and Third Partitions. From them you will gather that almost any disease of the mind or body can be traced to, or influenced by, the cold and dry humour dominated by the planet Saturn. A quotation from a single small sub-section of the Synopsis of the First Partition (Burton's *Anatomy of Melancholy*, ed. Rev. A. R. Shilleto, Bell, 1896, Vol. I, p. 148), concerning Head-melancholy, perhaps relates most closely to the subjects of the first three of the poems under discussion.

Figure 6   Albrecht Dürer: Melencolia, 1617 (Mansell Collection)

Figure 6   Dürer's Melencolia (1514)
Commentary by Catherine King

Dürer's *Melencolia* is a very complex personification, and it invites complex analysis rightly, for Dürer wrote notes on little details and their meanings in early sketches – 'Key denotes power; purse denotes wealth' – and this refers to the purse and keys hanging from Melencolia's belt, which might seem rather insignificant details visually.

Panofsky has pointed out what an extraordinary personification it is – for the attributes of Geometry and Mathematics (the geometric solids, the compasses, the 'magic' square of numbers) have been added to those of Melancholy (the dog, the bat) and are accompanied by those of genius (the wings on Melancholy's shoulders, the wreath) and practical skill (the building and carpentry tools strewn on the floor).

What is Dürer saying? It's something very complex and, I think, not subject to a complete answer – and it's also very eccentric and personalized although it was to enter the tradition of the handbooks by the end of the sixteenth century. Three important general ideas underlie the meaning. Firstly, there is the tradition that Melancholy is a characteristic of those born under the influence of the planet Saturn, and that their disquiet – often leading to madness – results from their having too much 'black bile' – one of the four humours making up man's body.

The Melancholic is destined to unhappiness. Increasingly under the influence of neo-Platonism his madness was associated with the divine frenzy of inspiration which Plato had described as the characteristic of genius. This fitted in well with the older tradition that scholars and intellectuals were Saturnine – were melancholics. The Renaissance concept of genius is that it combines two things – inspiration or divine madness *and* practical skill: the first comes from God, the other can be learnt. Finally there is the neo-Platonic concept of knowledge which, following on Plato, sees knowledge as at its highest when it concentrates on the pure, mathematical and geometrical Reality behind appearances. The geometer, the mathematician, the architect – even the artist – deal with theory – with the laws of Nature. The seated woman has the wings of genius – the ability to rise above the ordinary concerns of 'Everyman' to the higher realities of geometrical, astronomical and mathematical study – to soar away from the ordinary world. This is the special prerogative of the scholar-genius. He is capable of creating things – buildings – ideas and so on – through his knowledge of the mathematical, Platonic principles governing all matter and his practical, learnt skill. But his potential is matched by his destined unhappiness. We might say – the more he knows, the more he knows what he doesn't know. His divine inspiration may turn imperceptibly to true madness – his confidence to self-consciousness and self-doubt. Panofsky sees the child as a symbol of mere ability to *learn* a skill; the woman's sad, introverted expression and behaviour as pure thought, unaccompanied by skill. Dürer's portrait of *Melencolia* is of a world out of joint: the genius weighed down by the knowledge that he cannot make the effort to use skilfully – or apply his practical experience to. Around *Melencolia* lie disused tools. The hourglass reminds us continually of Time passing. It's a picture of a complex dilemma: knowledge and skill, thought and action, with the ladder up to 'higher things' and the promise of the rainbow in a sunny sky far removed.

The personifications you've seen in Unit 11 on *Iconography* were, traditionally, of a very simple sort, seldom betraying or expressing much complex psychology or personal feelings. This is different. The figure of Melencolia is *not* just a figure with attributes – like a rather neutral signboard. She's characterized and the whole engraving is full of the same uneasy emotion as the intense face. The personification too, is probably personal. Dürer had enthusiastically adopted the Italian idea that the artist was an intellectual. He had tried, was trying, to *create* beauty through mathematical means – through calculating proportion and so on. *Melencolia* might be seen as a statement of the conflicts involved in this enterprise: the difficulties of harmonizing thought and practice, ambition and action, inspiration with common sense. Ultimately it seems to be about the two faces of Saturn – the divine frenzy and the threat of madness. In this sense it is a very new use of personification, and artistic symbolism in general. (The references to Elizabethan melancholy in the poetry you will be reading will be much more diluted – possibly less than Dürer's etching expresses.)

4.13 (continued)

Head-melancholy Sub. I

In body
Headache, binding, heaviness, vertigo, lightness, singing of the ears, much waking, fixed eyes, high colour, red eyes, hard belly, dry body, no great sign of melancholy in the other parts.

or

In mind
Continual fear, sorrow, suspicion, discontent, superfluous cares, solicitude, anxiety, perpetual cogitation of such toys they are possessed with, thoughts like dreams, etc.

The supposedly medical basis for such thinking was derived from the theories first set forth by Hippocrates (probably fl. second half of fifth century B.C.), and developed by Galen (A.D. 129–c. 200), and need not detain us. More to our purpose is the Renaissance emphasis upon an observation attributed to Aristotle 'that all those who have become eminent in philosophy or politics or poetry or the arts are clearly melancholics' (quoted by Bridget Gellert Lyons, *Voices of Melancholy*, Routledge & Kegan Paul, 1971, p. 3). A little melancholy was thought to be essential to the man of wit and sensibility, but excess of it was considered ruinous to health and conduct. Hamlet is the best-known example of a character exhibiting a wide range of melancholic qualities, including *Love-Melancholy*, which, together with Jealousy 'a bastard-branch, or Kind of Love-Melancholy', occupies three hundred and fifty-seven pages of my edition of Burton. Bridget Gellert Lyons has a whole chapter (Chapter Four), and J. Dover Wilson (*What Happens in Hamlet*, Cambridge, 1935) an Appendix (E), devoted to Hamlet as a melancholic. Have a look at the painting (c. 1610–5) by Isaac Oliver of one of England's most famous and intellectual young nobles, Lord Herbert of Cherbury, in the attitude of the melancholy knight (Figure 7). Armour and mount discarded, he lies pensively in the woods besides a stream, his only arms a sword and a shield labelled MAGICA SYMPATHIA. Catherine King writes: ' "Magical sympathy" was thought to offer protection, sympathetic magic being a means of draining down the influence of the heavens to counteract the dangers of being dominated by Saturn, the planet which disposed people to melancholy.' You can imagine how completely acceptable ideas about melancholy would have to become for such a person to commission such a portrait of himself.

Figure 7   Isaac Oliver: Miniature of Edward Herbert, 1st Baron of Cherbury as a melancholy knight (c. 1610) (Powis Castle)

Now please read the four poems, making notes, as with previous poems, on

(i)   subject

(ii)   mood or tone

(iii) style or presentation.

Please try also to explain why, following my practice with poems on Time, and on Death, I place the Jonson poem last of this group.

DISCUSSION

4.14   *The world's a bubble*

(i)   The common feature most notably absent from this poem of lamentation about the vicissitudes of earthly life is the conventional religious hope of a better hereafter. No 'Mount we unto the sky' here. The poet rejects not just the three conventional social targets of the satirist – court, country and city life in the second stanza – but everything else, including marriage, offspring, exploration, war and peace. It is a faintly incredible performance, more worthy of a puling adolescent than a philosopher and statesman; the most charitable explanation is that it might be a literary exercise – such as a poem of classical Cynic content. The last line is from Sophocles.

(ii)   As such, in it Bacon has well caught the savage mordant tone which Raleigh better demonstrates,

(iii) and his use of this rare stanza form is particularly felicitous. Note how the short lines gain epigrammatic and conclusive force by being rhymed with the longer preceding lines, and how in every case, the short line is heavily end-stopped. Note too, the sense of pattern the refrain-like couplets at the end of each stanza give to the whole poem. The bubble, by the way, was one of the favourite exemplars of Mutability.

4.15   *Care-charmer sleep*

(i)   A real Melancholy poem, this. I hope you turned at once to the short quotation from Burton which I gave you, and checked the content of the poem against it.

(ii)   You may know more personally moving poetry about Sleep, spoken by guilty (*Macbeth* II.ii) or careworn (*Henry IV*, Part Two, III.i) heroes; generalized and 'finely modulated pathos' (J. W. Lever, in *The Elizabethan Love Sonnet*, Methuen University Paperback, 1966, p. 154, thus characterizes Daniel's achievement in the *Delia* sonnet sequence) was a late Elizabethan desideratum in poetry and drama, which Daniel fulfils in this poem.

(iii) Points to note about the style. Nicely placed inversions of stress give pleasing variety to the flow (lines 2, 9, 11); harmonious and unobtrusive alliteration (lines 1, 2, 3, 7, 8, 9, 10, 12, 13, 14); enough obtrusive strong words and combinations to diversify the general tone of soft melancholy, and make the reader sit up ('dark forgetting', 'shipwreck', 'torment', 'liars', 'aggravate'). Daniel's influence (see Lucie-Smith's comment on p. 76 of your anthology) on his fellow-poets marks him as a man of the future for his style, a man of the present for his content. Contrast the *sound* and *tone* of his poetry with that of Raleigh's, by reading aloud, or by listening to the recordings we have made for you, or both.

4.16   *The Prologue from Antonio's Revenge*

I shan't discuss this popular invocation of appropriate audience attitude to a tragedy, but merely draw attention to two features. One is the savage pathetic fallacy in the opening description of Nature in winter ('Chilleth the wan bleak cheek of the numbed earth', 'snarling gusts', 'nak'd shuddering branch' and so forth), and the other is the extreme to which the doctrine of pathetic melancholy is taken in the body of the Prologue. Happiness positively disables 'apprehension' (which means judicious understanding) and the poet welcomes a playgoer who has 'a breast Nailed to the earth with grief'.

4.17   *To the world, a farewell for a gentlewoman, virtuous and noble*

(i)   Jonson manages in this conventional and highly formal elegy to combine many elements, among which I note:

(a)   Traditional medieval scorn of the world transmuted into precise social criticism;

(b)   A philosophical, quasi-religious argument against surrendering to the world;

(c)   A plea for emotional and intellectual integrity, which is implicit in the description of the world (the eight lines beginning 'Then, in a soil hast planted me');

(d)   Fortitude, acceptance of a world in which people suffer, and identification with fellow-sufferers ('But, what we are born for' and the eight lines following);

(e)   Final resolution to contain all discontents 'Here in my bosom, and at home'.

(ii)   It is hard to find the right words for the tone. 'Restrained censoriousness overlaid by high compassion'? No, that won't do. It is an example of the higher pathos, which does not fly into the rhetorical attitudes of either sensational description or passionate self-pity, but temperately states the causes, and accepts the facts, of 'age, misfortune, sickness, grief', all common gifts of Mutability.

(iii)   The poignancy of the poem is increased by its dependence on a particular character, the 'Gentlewoman, Virtuous and Noble' of the title.

I placed this poem last because, as with the last poems of previous groups, I consider it the best, and because you may need something of a corrective to the impression which you may have gained from all these Mutability poems, that Elizabethan poetry has nothing to offer in the face of vicissitude but musical and self-pitying screams. Though it is cast in the form of a conventional rejection of the world, this is an *anti*-Melancholy poem, because the essence of Melancholy is excess, which Jonson fundamentally despises.

5.0   MUSIC

First, study the diagram from Gafurius' *Practica Musicae* (Figure 8), and Catherine King's commentary.

5.1   If everything Elizabethan man could see was a 'hierogliphick' or 'emblem' of God's glory, then everything he could hear was a sound-emblem of the same. Music above all had a special place in the world order, of which there were three aspects. You know already about Degree, the system of ranking everything in nature within its particular category, and about Allegory, the means of relating different aspects of existence in correspondence and meaning. The Cosmic Dance was the third aspect, and the poem which best expresses it is Sir John Davies' *Orchestra*, about one-seventh of which appears in your anthology (pp. 86–90). In this section, I shall lead up to the study of those nineteen stanzas, through a little of the history of the ideas contained in them, and through one or two poems and prose passages which will help to set the mood, and the climate of thought and feeling, in which Elizabethans approached music.

5.2 First of all, turn to Lorenzo's music-inspired love-talk to Jessica in the garden scene from *The Merchant of Venice* (p. 222). Read it carefully, bearing in mind that this is not just a lover's fancy, but a formulation of orthodox ideas about a universe with the profoundest ordered purposes of which the lover, being in the ecstasy of love, feels himself in harmony.

5.3 **DISCUSSION**

As so often Shakespeare bases himself on current ideas, but achieves a new synthesis. First of all, there is the doctrine of the music of the spheres which Plato took over from Pythagoras, as it was transmitted and transmuted by Plotinus; by the mystic whose writings circulated under the authority of Dionysius the Areopagite, but who was in fact a fourth- or fifth-century Christian neo-Platonist; and by such Renaissance philosophers as Ficino. Pagan and Christian alike had developed an idea which is often found in religion – that the creation and working of the universe are harmonious and mathematically proportioned, and therefore musical, manifestations of the divine mind. You have seen how this musical harmony worked in relation to architecture and to proportion in the human body, in Units 8–11. In some religions, such as Hinduism, the act of creation itself is seen as a dance, and an illuminating Judaeo-Christian reference, which I think explains why Shakespeare does not follow the exact terminology approved by Neo-Platonists, is in the book of Job:

> Whereupon are the foundations thereof [i.e. of the earth – B.S.] fastened? or who laid the corner stone thereof; When the morning stars sang together, and all the sons of God shouted for joy?
>
> *Job*, 38, 6–7, Authorized Version.

In Plato, each sphere made its own note; the stars themselves did not sing. But Shakespeare's and Job's did. The fact that Shakespeare treats of the perpetual motion of the spheres, and Job of the creation, is of minor importance. Without tracing the detailed ideas about cosmic harmony as they developed before and during our period, or bothering whether pagan sirens or Christian angels were the makers of divine music, I ask you to accept, in reading these poems:

(a)   Music as a reflection of the divine harmony, and hence almost divine itself;

(b)   Absence of appreciation of music as a quality that in some way disabled the soul in its quest for heaven. As Lorenzo says later in the scene:

The man that hath no music in himself,
Nor is not mov'd with concord of sweet sounds,
Is fit for treasons, stratagems, and spoils;
The motions of his spirit are dull as night,
And his affections dark as Erebus.

The Merchant of Venice, V.i.82–6, in *William Shakespeare:*
the Complete Works, ed. P. Alexander, Collins, 1951.

5.4   The best English summary of (a) happens to be in the well-known words of
John Dryden (*A Song for St. Cecilia's Day*, 22 November 1687), and although
the poem is out of our period, I ask you to read its opening stanza now:

From Harmony, from heav'nly Harmony
  This universal Frame began;
When Nature underneath a heap
Of jarring Atomes lay,
And cou'd not heave her Head,
The tuneful Voice was heard from high,
  Arise, ye more than dead.
Then cold and hot and moist and dry
In order to their Stations leap,
  And MUSICK'S pow'r obey.
From Harmony, from heav'nly Harmony
  This universal Frame began:
    From Harmony to Harmony
Through all the Compass of the Notes it ran,
The Diapason closing full in Man.

The Poems of John Dryden, ed. John Sargeaunt, Oxford University Press, 1913, p. 196.

And some implications of (b) above, relating it to problems of the dual nature
of Man, as both corruptible and perfectible, appear in Bacon's gloss (1605)
on the story of Orpheus, a myth which, it will not surprise you to learn, was
highly popular with Elizabethans.

> Neither is certainly that other merit of learning, in repressing the inconveniences which
> grow from man to man, much inferior to the former, of relieving the necessities which
> arise from nature; which merit was lively set forth by the ancients in that feigned relation
> of Orpheus' theatre, where all beasts and birds assembled; and forgetting their several
> appetites, some of prey, some of game, some of quarrel, stood all sociably together
> listening unto the airs and accords of the harp; the sound whereof no sooner ceased,
> or was drowned by some louder noise, but every beast returned to his own nature:
> wherein is aptly described the nature and condition of men, who are full of savage and
> unreclaimed desires, of profit, of lust, of revenge; which as long as they give ear to
> precepts, to laws, to religion, sweetly touched with eloquence and persuasion of books,
> sermons of harangues, so long is society and peace maintained; but if these instruments[1]
> be silent, or that sedition and tumult make them not audible, all things dissolve into
> anarchy and confusion.

[1] i.e. of 'precepts . . . harangues'

The Advancement of Learning and New Atlantis, ed. Case,
Oxford University Press, 1906 reprinted 1960, pp. 51–2.

5.5   You will have noticed that Lorenzo believes that mere humans cannot hear
the music of the spheres. That bliss is reserved for perfected souls, who may
then join the Dance of the Blessed. As you can readily imagine, there are
hierarchies of music, as of other created things. Devils as well as angels play
music; their tunes and rhythms excite corruptible, and especially concupiscible,
man, and when devils triumph through their evil disharmony, the lost souls
join the Dance of Death, and then the Dance of the Damned. The subject is a
huge one, which I cannot deal with here. If you are interested, such a book as
The Music of the Spheres and The Dance of Death, by Kathi Meyer-Baer (Princeton
University Press, 1970), will tell you most of what you wish to know, and give

you one more range of insights to help you in your appreciation and understanding of medieval and Renaissance literary and visual arts. My aim here is to give you enough background to enrich your understanding of the poetry in which music figures.

5.6   Educators of the age made an explicit connection between the symbolism of music, and practical music as it figured in a gentleman's education and normal accomplishments. Here is a jingle about the trivium and quadrivium quoted by Maurice Hussey in his useful little book *The World of Shakespeare and his Contemporaries: a Visual Approach* (Heinemann, 1971, pp. 15–16). It is taken from Thomas Wilson's *Rule of Reason* (1551):

> GRAMMAR doth teach to utter words,
> To speak both apt and plain.
> LOGIC by art sets forth the truth
> And tells us what is vain.
> RHETORIC at large paints well the cause,
> And makes that seem right gay
> Which LOGIC spake but a word
> And taught us by the way.
> MUSIC with tunes delights the ear
> And makes us think of heaven.
> ARITHMETIC by number can make
> Reckonings be even.
> GEOMETRY things thick and broad
> Measures by line and square.
> ASTRONOMY by stars doth tell
> Of foul and eke of fair.

Figure 8   Diagram: Practica Musicae *1496*
Commentary by Catherine King

This diagram comes from Gafurius' treatise on music: *Practica Musicae*. It shows how mythology (Apollo and the Muses), cosmography (Earth composed of fire (Ignis), air (Aer), earth (Terra) and water (Aqua) below the seven planets and the celestial sphere of fixed stars (celum stellatum)) and music (the octave's tones and semitones and the Greek modes (types of scales) – Phrygian, Lydian etc.) were welded in the minds of Renaissance intellectuals into a total (though very unscientific) world view. Each of the planets corresponds to the seven spheres and the sphere of the stars. The ninth Muse 'Thalia' is associated with Earth – to neaten the diagram.

Each Muse and planet is further associated with a particular mode and a particular tone or semitone. The whole is joined by the serpent of Eternity to Apollo in the heavens, who is shown with his companions, the Three Graces, and is holding the lute with which he tamed the animals. The legend above his head reads 'The strength of Apollo moves the Muses universally' – that is, the universe which Plato, in his *Timaeus*, said was constructed according to the mathematical ratios of the musical octave, and moves in a harmony similar to that of music.

*Figure 8
(facing page)
Apollo, the planets, the
Muses and the modes, from
Franchinus Gafurius
Practica Musicae, 1496
(Cambridge University
Library)*

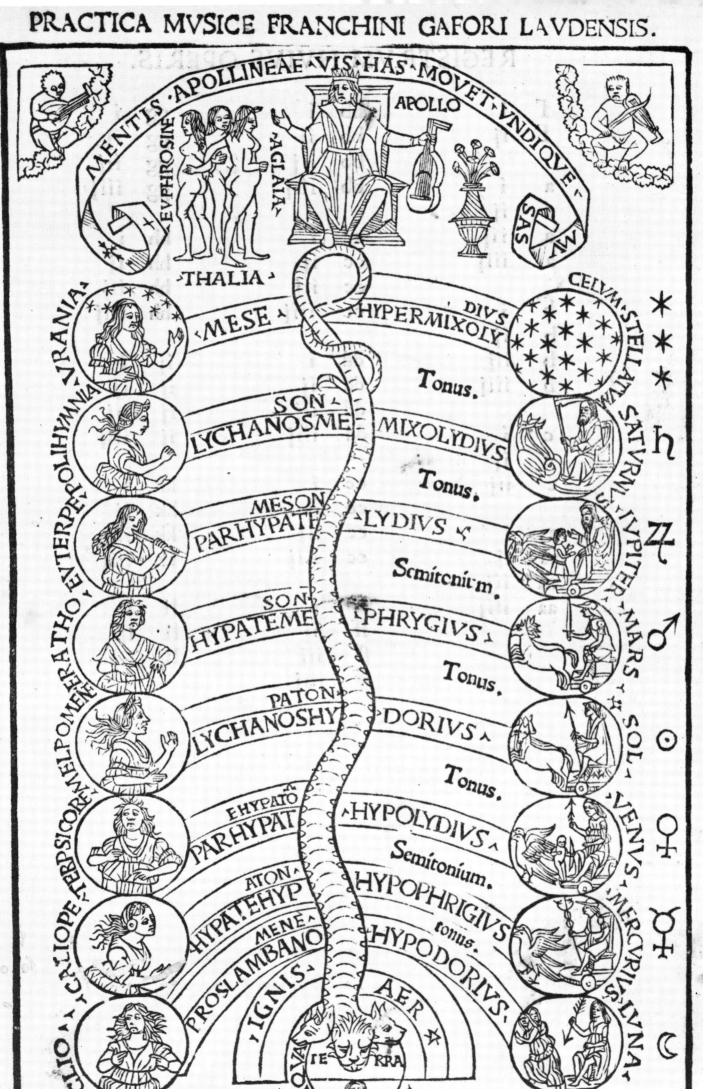

MENTIS·APOLLINEAE·VIS·HAS·MOVET·VNDIQVE·MVSAS

EVPHROSINE · AGLAIA · THALIA · APOLLO

VRANIA · POLIHYMNIA · ERATHO · MELPOMENE · TERPSICORE · CALIOPE · CLIO

MESE · SON LYCHANOSME · MESON PARHYPATE · SON HYPATEME · PATON LYCHANOSHY · EHYPATO PARHYPAT · ATON HYPATEHYP · MENE PROSLAMBANO

DIVS HYPERMIXOLY
Tonus.
MIXOLYDIVS
Tonus.
LYDIVS
Semitonium.
PHRYGIVS
Tonus.
DORIVS
Tonus.
HYPOLYDIVS
Semitonium.
HYPOPHRIGIVS
tonus.
HYPODORIVS

CELVM·STELLATVM·SATVRNI·IVPITER·MARS·SOL·VENVS·MERCVRIVS·LVNA

IGNIS · AER · AQVA · TERRA

5.7   Now, to make an explicit and effective relation between music and poetry, read Richard Barnfield's 'If music and sweet poetry agree' (p. 45 of your anthology). It will make an appropriate motto poem for the gramophone record accompanying Units 29 and 30, on which both song and poetry will figure. As you read it, make notes on

(i)   the successive aspects of Elizabethan artistic and cultural life which you find in it (not all of which, by the way, have been raised in this study material so far), and

(ii)   comment on the prevailing sentiment.

5.8   **DISCUSSION**

(i)   Poetry and music as sister arts (lines 1–2);
Correspondence between these arts and love (lines 3–4);
Love as a Platonic and aesthetic concern (implicit throughout);
Dowland and Spenser as the masters of the respective arts (lines 5–8);

Music as a ravisher of the senses (line 6);
Poetry as 'deep conceit' (line 7);
Music as the song of a god (lines 11–12);
The lute as the characteristic instrument for ravishing the soul (lines 6 and 10), on account of the myth of Orpheus and his lute;
Platonic compliment (lines 13–14) in the modern, i.e. asexual sense.

(ii)   The prevailing tone derives from all the above, but the Platonic compliment is especially characteristic of the Elizabethan age. It is the use of the word 'love' between men, or between poets and patronesses, in Elizabethan poetry, which so distinguishes the age from ours. We have lost the use of the word outside a sexual, or specifically religious, frame of reference, and do not have the inherently neo-Platonic feeling for 'love' as essentially a beautiful state of human grace which may apply among people, or between humans and God. Part of Peter Bembo's address on Love in the Fourth Book of Baldassare Castiglione's *Il Cortegiano* (translated by Sir Thomas Hoby, 1561, as *The Book of the Courtier*), perhaps the most important of all Renaissance neo-Platonist works, may here give you some notion of the concept:

> What tongue mortall is there then (O most holy love) that can sufficiently prayse thy worthines? Thou most beautifull, most good, most wise, art derived of the unitie of the heavenly beautie, goodnesse and wisdom, and therein dost thou abide, and unto it through it, (as in a circle) turnest about.
> Thou the most sweete bond of the world, a meane betwixt heavenly and earthly thinges, with a bountifull temper bendest the high vertues to the government of the lower, and turning backe the mindes of mortall men to their beginning, couplest them with it.
> Thou with agreement bringest the Elements in one, stirrest nature to bring forth, and that which ariseth and is borne for the succession of the life. Thou bringest severed matters into one, to the unperfect givest perfection, to the unlike likenesse, to enimitie amitie, to the earth fruites, to the Sea calmnesse, to the heaven, lively light.
> Thou art the father of true pleasures, of grace, peace, lowlinesse, and good will, enimy to rude wildnesse, and sluggishnesse: to be short, the beginning, and end of all goodnesse. And forsomuch as thou delightest to dwell in the floure of beautifull bodies and beautifull soules, I suppose that thy abiding place is now here among us, and from above otherwhile shewest thy selfe a litle to the eyes and mindes of them that bee not worthie to see thee.
>
> Dent, 1928, reprinted 1966, p. 321.

Bear that passage in mind both when you come to the love poems in the next section, and now, when you turn to *Orchestra*.

6.0 *ORCHESTRA* BY SIR JOHN DAVIES

6.1   The word 'orchestra' in Greek meant 'dancing-floor'. The extract from *Orchestra* (p. 86 of your anthology) comprises stanzas 34–52, or most of the section (stanzas 32–60) to which the poet gives the description, 'The speech of Love persuading men to learn dancing'. When the poem was re-published in 1622, it was sub-titled 'A poem expressing the antiquity and excellence of dancing, in a dialogue between Penelope and one of her wooers: not finished'. 'The antiquity and excellence of dancing' was widely accepted: Sir Thomas Elyot, in *The Boke Named The Governour*, a treatise on education and politics dedicated to Henry VIII and published in 1531, prominently recommends dancing, a recommendation of which his descendant, T. S. Eliot, makes use by quoting from Chapter XXI of Book I of *The Governour* in the first section of *East Coker* (*Four Quartets*, Faber, 1944, p. 16):

> The association of man and woman
> In daunsinge, signifying matrimonie –
> A dignified and commodious sacrament.
> Two and two, necessarye coniunction,
> Holding eche other by the hand or the arm
> Whiche betokeneth concorde.

That description is highly relevant to *Orchestra*, the central situation of which is the attempt of Antinous, most reputable of Penelope's suitors during Odysseus' absence, to persuade her to dance, and so, by implication, to give him her heart.

6.2   The poem begins lyrically and almost playfully, as Davies chides Homer for having omitted to describe the 'courtly love' which 'Antinous, that fresh and jolly knight', made to Queen Penelope. Then Davies sets to work, and describes Penelope, transfigured by Pallas Athene into a special state of beauty because she hoped to hear the 'sweet singer Phemius' refer to her husband in song. Antinous is moved to ask her to dance and so imitate the motion of heaven, but she declines, calling dancing 'this new rage'. A disputation in formal style has begun. Antinous relates the pedigree of dancing; it has come from the brain of love, the power that can resolve chaos and disorder by showing souls the musical structure and motion of the universe. Love's account of this, as related by Antinous, is the subject of your study.

6.3   Before I ask you to read the poem, I must tell you how, though 'not finished', it proceeds from this point to the conclusion. (If you'd rather find out for yourself, the full poem appears in the Everyman *Silver Poets of the Sixteenth Century*, and all except the final detached group of five stanzas, describing dancing at the court of Queen Elizabeth, appears in *The Oxford Book of Sixteenth Century Verse*.) Antinous, who throughout, as pleader, carries the burden of the debate, tells Penelope how Love taught men to dance, and enumerates and characterizes the different sorts of dance – 'rounds or country dances', 'measures', 'galliards', 'corantos', and 'lavoltas' are the poet's narrative subtitles. Then he proceeds to 'grace in dancing' and 'the use and forms of dancing in sundry affairs of man's life', which include the arts of peace and war, triumphs, funerals and the liberal arts (stanzas 92–6 make a splendid lyrical gloss to Thomas Wilson's dreary fourteen lines explaining the trivium and quadrivium). Penelope rejects the whole of Antinous' argument, presenting, in opposition to his ideal view, love as lust and destruction. Antinous' rejoinder is that he is speaking of true love – in effect, the kind of love about which Bembo rhapsodizes in *The Book of the Courtier* – which he finds reflected in Penelope herself:

> Love in the twinkling of your eyelids danceth,
> Love danceth in your pulses and your veins,
> Love, when you sew, your needle's point advanceth
> And makes it dance a thousand curious strains
> Of winding rounds, whereof the form remains,
> To show that your fair hands can dance the hay,
> Which your fine feet would learn as well as they.
>
> (stanza 106)

> Sir John Davies, *Orchestra, or a Poem of Dancing* ed. E. M. W. Tillyard, Chatto and Windus, 1945, p. 41.

Concord and Comeliness, Antinous says, are the characteristics of dance. But the argument does not move Penelope, and Antinous is forced to call on Love himself, who appears with a mirror in which Penelope sees a vision of the moon enthroned, surrounded by dancing stars, though Vulcan, maker of the mirror, had there represented 'Our glorious English court's divine image'. 'Penelope, rapt with sweet pleasure', yields to the persuasion of the beneficent vision, but the poem breaks off before she can yield in her own corresponding situation, to her importunate suitor. Decorum has been preserved, and a wittily grandiloquent compliment paid to the old unmarried queen.

Davies dedicated the poem 'To his very friend, Master Richard Martin', a fellow-student at the Middle Temple. But not long after, resenting Martin's satirical opposition over some discussion, he entered the dining room between two men armed with swords and broke a cudgel on Martin's head, for which he was disbarred. *Orchestra* must have been written before Davies was twenty-five, and it took him, according to his dedicatory sonnet, only fifteen days to compose.

6.4   The single question I should like you to answer as you read the extract from *Orchestra*, is:

Taking the neo-Platonic mechanism as much in your stride as you can – because, after all, you must know it well by now, and if you don't, your editor provides most of what you need to know in this note to the poem on page 278 – in brief note form write an appreciation, supporting your comments on subject, language, tone and so forth with evidence. (It will help if before reading you number the stanzas, from 1 to 19. In the discussion following, I can then place references easily and quickly.)

But please don't let your task obscure your total response to the poem. Before making your notes, I should read it straight through for the meaning and the music, and to get the rhythm and pattern of the rhyme royal impressed on your mind.

6.5   **DISCUSSION**

I want first of all to make a single statement describing the extract from the poem, which I will then support by detailed discussion:

The ruling principle of the poem is motion. This motion is activated, as it were, by a sensuous and strongly physical apprehension of the

different attributes of nature, of which the human body and the heavenly bodies are chief. The informing emotion is love, passionately and even mystically inherent in all nature.

6.6 It is a pity that, lacking the whole poem, you cannot see all this in its full context of story and compliment. Let me now try to justify what I have written.

Motion. It is not just that the whole poem is a dance, and that words of motion are everywhere, as elements in a great plan of *fixed* creative harmony, that is so striking. I list the words of motion in stanzas 1 and 3. (1: whirled, whirled, wandering, dance; 3: disordered, scattered, movings, return, break.) Make your own list for stanzas 14 and 19. Note the many examples of *ordered* mutability, and refresh your memory, if you need to, by referring back to the Spenser discussion (Section 3).

The Human Body. In fact, a group of people is addressed in the 'you' of stanza 1. The eyes are *quick*, one of a host of words which reflect the poet's sense of the vividness and activity of life. Venus dancing to the sun (stanza 14) and Echo, dancing to other people's voices, are sensuous women, and so is the land of stanza 16. Lastly, in stanzas 18 and 19 the whole physical earth becomes the fertile body of a woman flowing with 'sweet fresh moisture'. But more important than all these, *dance*, the fundamental subject of the poem, is appropriate to the human body, and so whenever other kinds of motion in the universe are described as dancing, every dancer, whether wave or star, is subtly metamorphosed into a human being.

The Heavenly Bodies I can leave safely to you. But as you go over them, please notice the constant personification, sometimes amounting to anthropomorphism, in Davies' description of them.

Love as the Informing Emotion. It is not enough simply to list the love words and love activities in the poem, but that gives us a start. Examples are: the king and queen of stanza 4, Venus dancing to the sun in stanza 5, father and mother and the reveller and his leman in stanza 6, the coy moon in stanza 8, the air *embracing* rules in stanza 14, the sea clipping (a strong Elizabethan love-word, meaning to embrace passionately) the land in stanza 16, and the waves kissing the shore in stanza 17. What is important is to enter the poet's vision of dancing as the fundamental love activity, a love which shows equally in the creative power of the heavens to make and sustain a beautiful universe, and in the living power of all natural phenomena to manifest beauty and harmony in their being and doing. In this context, mention in stanza 9 of the lame and ugly god Vulcan and his attribute of creative fire varies the general harmony with a winning and sympathetic paradox.

Passionately and Mystically. Enough of passion; I think such a poem as this would be rather boring if it were not for the mystical feeling of the poet for his material. He spiritualizes it by investing it with qualities of divine meaning and force, always aspiring to levels of intensity and comprehension beyond human reach. And the vehicle remains the fundamental metaphor of the dance. Consider for a moment the stanzas which deal with air and wind movement (10, 11, 14). Does not a feeling for the superhuman underlie the fancy upon which they are based? But the poet, though 'religious' in the accepted Elizabethan style, is not making an explicitly religious point; he does not see neo-Platonic and Christian ideas about the universe as far apart, though to us the neo-Platonic attitude was distinctive.

6.7 To end this discussion, it will be fruitful for you to compare the different ecstatic senses of Davies, as he describes the heavens (stanzas 1–4), and Vaughan, a religious poet of slightly later date, as he contemplates them, in the first stanza of what is perhaps his best-known poem, *The World* (1650):

> I saw Eternity the other night
> Like a great *Ring* of pure and endless light,
>   All calm, as it was bright,
> And round beneath it, Time in hours, days, years
>   Driv'n by the spheres
> Like a vast shadow mov'd, In which the world
>   And all her train were hurl'd;
> The doting Lover in his queintest strain
>   Did their Complain,
> Neer him, his Lute, his fancy, and his flights,
>   Wits sour delights,
> With gloves, and knots the silly snares of pleasure
>   Yet his dear Treasure
> All scatter'd lay, while he his eys did pour
>   Upon a flowr.

> *Poetry and Selected Prose of Henry Vaughan*, ed. L. C. Martin
> Oxford University Press, 1963, p. 299.

That stanza, with its daunting swoop from pondering eternity to contemplating a flower, and its grave moral conspectus, represents the best of English mystical poetry about the universe. It should help you, largely by contrast, to evaluate Davies' philosophy of life, and his poetic achievement. (There is a short general essay on Davies in Alpers, pp. 321–6, by T. S. Eliot, who, however, deals mainly with Davies' other well-known poem, *Nosce Teipsum* (Know Thyself).)

7–8   LOVE

The volume and variety of Elizabethan love poetry are immense, and in the short time available for study I shall not try to represent all its main elements, or even to describe the genre in general terms. Taking your anthology as a basis, and adding to it a few carefully chosen poems, I want to help you to build on the knowledge of Elizabethan poetry you have acquired so far; and if, as I hope, that new knowledge has already brought you a liking for the poetry of the period, then extension of that liking into love poetry should follow naturally and bring your fortnight's work to a culmination. Love poetry, like the poetry of religious autobiography, in which poets of a slightly later period excel, is a field in which, commonly, intense and personal experience is expressed. In the proposed culmination, the love poetry of Shakespeare, in his sonnets, will predominate. My two aims, which contrast sharply, are:

(i)   To give you as much reading of the poetry as possible, with only absolutely necessary guidance before you read, and limited comment, sometimes amounting to no more than selective annotation, after you have done the reading.

(ii)   To offer detailed work on a few poems, as a means of establishing in your mind the kind of achievement of which Elizabethan poets were capable.

7.1   First, a group of poems, some of which are songs, and most of which draw their subject matter and some of their inspiration from popular life, folk-lore and romance. It is worth pausing to consider your attitude to popular literature before going on. The study of literature is mostly concerned with the work of great writers, while popular literature, whether oral or written (and strictly speaking, 'oral literature' is a contradiction in terms), tends to be the province of social historians, folk-lorists and anthropologists. But popular literature is included in literary studies for any of three main reasons: one, that it is 'good enough' as literature to deserve study for its own sake; two, that the evidence it provides about life is essential for study of the literature of a given period or country; and three, that its influence on authors studied, or its use by them as source material, renders incidental study of it necessary. Cicely Havely and I have had to judge this matter finely, in the light of our central problem of having only two weeks for Elizabethan poetry on this course. We decided, as you know, to allot both radio programmes for these units to popular poetry.

7.2   By way of supplement I include here a few love-poems, most of which are by known authors, and most of which draw upon popular culture. Each poem so chosen is 'good enough' though none, except possibly those by Peele, will stand comparison with the lyric masterpieces of the age.

Also as supplement in this broad category, I am including on the accompanying gramophone record a few songs. But, for reasons of economy, I have had to limit these to those set for solo voice and lute. And a further limitation placed on me was the virtual absence of contemporary settings of love-songs from the plays. This is particularly regrettable, because it is clear from the way drama-tists planned the songs and other musical entries in their plays that music was both integral and important in their dramatic conceptions. All we really know from texts and stage directions is the words of songs, the number of singers (sometimes), the kinds of instruments used for different occasions, and the kinds of musical entries. The consolation that remains is the excellence of the lyrics of many of the songs, and it is with a group of these that I ask you to begin.

7.3   These songs and song-like poems (pp. 205–6 of your anthology) are taken from George Peele's *The Old Wives' Tale*, which was probably written in about 1591. It is a mainly prose play of only 925 lines, in which Peele satirizes the popular romantic drama and such aspects of the literary scene as Stanyhurst's monstrous attempts to adapt English poetry to classical metre and Latin linguistic patterns. The romantic elements of the play, which are narrated or set by an old woman called Madge before her husband, Clunch the smith, and three pages, include: a Wandering Knight in search of a Maiden who has been Abducted by a Conjuror; Two Brothers who become enchanted by the Conjuror while searching for the Abducted Maiden; a Slashing Knight; a Young Lover transformed into an Old Man; a Ghost called Jack; an Unhappy Father possessing two daughters, one beautiful and shrewish, the other ugly and virtuous; and the Well of Life complete with Talking Heads. The songs and the song-like spells reflect a mood of pure romance rather than the satirical purpose of the author in writing the whole play: this is important because it tells us that music and lyric poetry were important enough to Elizabethans for them always to be ready to diversify the current purpose with a golden moment of music, or poetry, or both.

7.4   Here are some notes on the four poems. In each case, read the notes first, then the poem, and then my commentary; and if the latter breaks new ground for you, then read the poem again in the light of it.

When as the rye reach to the chin   It is sung at the beginning of the play, before any of the romantic plot starts, as the first social activity when, the three pages having arrived at Clunch's house, Madge brings in cheese and pudding of her own making.

Be not afraid of every stranger   This is a spell of good advice delivered by the Old Man to the two questing brothers because they give him alms when they find him gathering sticks. The 'one flame of fire' is the flame burning under a hill which gives the Conjuror Sacrapant his power. The 'white bear of England's wood' is Merlin, the magician who counselled King Arthur.

Spread, table, spread   This charm is spoken by Sacrapant to produce a magical meal for Delya, the Abducted Maiden. Your editor's note implies that seduction was intended as part of abduction. The black cock is generally associated with supernatural evil, and the red with sexual power.

Gently dip but not too deep   The two girls, Zantippa the Curst (but beautiful) Daughter and Celanta the Fowle (but virtuous) Wench, come in turn to the Well of Life and hear this incantation spoken by the Head. Zantippa breaks the pitcher on the Head before it has finished speaking, and is given the deaf slashing knight Huanebango as a lover, which appals her. But Celanta hears it out, and gains riches for herself and her impoverished lover, Corebus. Read your editor's notes, to which I shall add in the commentary.

7.5   Commentary

Be not afraid of every stranger stands a little apart from the other three poems, in being related to love only through the quest element, and so I shall deal with it separately first. The basis of the action underlying the words is the folk theme of Hospitality Rewarded: good characters give charity to the seemingly destitute, who turn out to be powerful people in disguise or under spell, or possessors of hidden knowledge or second sight. Notice how the third and fourth lines, which are each trochaic but lack the final syllable, stand out because of this difference and because of their more strongly marked rhythm. They contain the core of the mysterious message, which is made more mysterious still by the attribution of the wisdom it contains to a person, Merlin, who is described only by circumlocution.

7.6   The song *When as the rye reach to the chin* is one of a huge number of spring and summer songs linking the season with desire. You may object that cherries and strawberries ripen earlier than a cereal crop like rye, but Peele probably means by 'rye' almost any long grass at hay-making time. 'Chop-cherry' or 'bob-cherry' is a game in which contestants try to eat cherries which are dangling from a string, without using their hands. Like 'barley-break', which you will meet a little later, it was one of a host of seasonal games which could be adapted to exciting courting purposes, such as, for example, by playing it for kisses. To 'chop the cherry' had as obvious a sexual sense as to 'pluck the rose'. The power of this little poem lies in its quite beautiful construction and sensibility. Each of the first four lines presents the plenty and joy of the summer in its own separate action picture, which is of a universal or general kind – the rye reaches to everyone's chin, everyone can play chop-cherry, strawberries everywhere are swimming in the cream, and schoolboys everywhere are playing in the stream. Then there comes the unique, three-times-repeated cry of one girl who is longing to be loved, and is moved intensely towards love by the atmosphere of the season. The long line with the 'O's (your editor modernizes: Peele wrote 'O') and the two short concluding lines, break the poetic mould established at the outset, and the prosaic simplicity of

Till that time come again
She could not live a maid

makes the hyperbolic assertion it expresses both sober and credible, a natural result of the poetic intoxication of the first four lines. You should always look closely when Elizabethan poets or dramatists write 'O', because they rarely use it as a mere gap-filler: here, the wild intensity of the threefold repetition raises and concentrates the emotional pitch of the poem, and provides a transition to the concluding revelatory statement.

7.7   *Spread, table, spread*   No further comment.

7.8   *Gently dip but not too deep* is a mysterious poem in which the bearded corn, the well of life, and some kind of fertility gods seem to be part of a ceremony which will ensure reward and happy love for the celebrant. Two stage directions which your editor does not include complete the meaning of the poem. Before the first stanza is spoken, 'A head comes up with eares of Corne, and she combes them in her lap', and before the second stanza is spoken, 'A head comes up fulle of golde, she combes it into her lap' (The Yale Edition of the *Life and Works of George Peele*, 1970, vol. III, p. 415). That is beautiful, and symbolic, and appropriate to pastoral poetry and masque – after all, it was 'the Queenes Maiesties players' who performed *The Old Wives' Tale*. But don't forget your editor's note on 'cockle-bread'; and add to it this from W. J. Thoms: *Anecdotes and Traditions*, London, 1839, vol. 5, pp. 94–5, in which the author quotes from a manuscript of the seventeenth-century antiquary, John Aubrey:

> Young wenches have a wanton sport which they call moulding of Cockle-bread, viz. they get upon a table-board, and then gather up their knees and their coates with their hands as high as they can, and then they wabble to and fro, as if they were kneading of dowgh, and say these words, viz.
>
> My dame is sick and gone to bed,
> And I'le go mould my Cockle-bread.

Aubrey mentions that in England before the Conquest, young women suspected of adultery might be asked if they had been moulding bread between their buttocks, and giving it to men.

But for all that stark anthropological detail, which I include because it is sometimes necessary to correct the impression that Elizabethan love poetry is all air and fire, it is Peele's transforming power as a poet that makes this little work haunting and beautiful. Consider the soft but elemental sensuousness of such lines as

Comb me smooth, and stroke my head;

and the rhythmical fascination, the profound and resonant moral suggestion of the theme instruction:

Gently dip, but not too deep.

Though you would scan those two lines similarly, in the latter, the short vowels of 'dip' and 'not', both of which bear main accentuation, help to give the line an entirely different rhythm.

Lastly, allow the concluding promise of riches, from hair to sheaf, from sheaf to golden tree, to take shape visually, in your mind's eye.

7.9   Peele is the only poet whose songs I would allow to stand beside Shakespeare's. The reason why I do not include material on *Bethsabe's Song* is that it figured in the Arts Foundation Course, which many of you will have studied. For those who did not, the poem is there in your book.

8.0   Now, a group of poems for quick reading, with introductory notes where necessary, but no subsequent commentary. In two of them you will recognize Burton's 'Love Melancholy'.

Arise, get up, my dear (p. 25)

'Bride-lace' was a piece of lace used to bind up the sprigs of rosemary worn at weddings (rosemary, ros marinus, meaning 'sea-dew'; an attribute of Venus and therefore propitious for love-making; an evergreen plant, its meaning in flower-language is fidelity in love).

'Firk': your editor's note is insufficient. The verb was widely used, both transitively and intransitively, to describe sudden, brisk movement, mostly in musical and love contexts.

Now is the month of maying (p. 27)

More musical love. Barley-break was a country game of pursuit played by three couples. The central couple of the three were said to be 'in hell', to which they could attract others by catching them, and since this involved embracing, or 'clipping' them, the game was often used as an erotic metaphor in literature, as in Herrick's 'Barly-Break: or, Last in Hell' (*The Poems of Robert Herrick*, Oxford University Press, 1933, reprinted 1951, p. 34).

> We two are last in Hell: what may we feare
> To be tormented, or kept Prisoners here?
> Alas! If kissing be of plagues the worst,
> We'll wish, in Hell we had been Last and First.

It is also referred to in one of your set plays, *The Changeling* (III.iii.172 and note, V.iii.163). The distinctly erotic Sidney poem to which Patricia Thomson refers, and which you may wish to look up either now or when you study that play, is 'A Shepheard's tale no height of style desires' (*The Poems of Sir Philip Sidney*, ed. W. A. Ringler Jr., Oxford University Press, 1962, pp. 242–56).

Weep you no more, sad fountains (p. 30)

Then these two poems, which are included for the lyric play they make with supernatural aspects of folk culture. The idea of an underground world inhabited by people of the past, used in the first poem, is common to many cultures. One English traditional belief is that King Arthur will one day ride out of his underground kingdom to resume his rule over an England which will then become an ideal country.

From *The wisdom of Doctor Dodipol* (p. 31)

Thrice toss these oaken ashes into air (p. 61)

A doleful fancy (p. 53)

Note how the trochaic rhythm, which is strong in the Church Latin of *Dies irae, dies illa*, the first line of the hymn on the Last Judgement used in requiem mass, suits the mood of musical melancholy. You'll meet it often in poetry; it is the rhythm of the Threnos from Shakespeare's *The phoenix and the turtle*, which I read in the short radio introduction to Unit 30, and which you'll find printed last of the additional poems. Compare *A doleful fancy* with *When thou must home* (p. 58), which you have already studied, and which is one of the finest songs of Love-Melancholy, uniting as it does the classical and medieval impulses: one of many songs in which Campion fulfilled his aim – 'I have chiefly aymed to couple my Words and Notes lovingly together' (*Poetry of the English Renaissance*, ed. J. W. Hebel and H. H. Hudson, 1938, pp. 444–5).

9.0   SIDNEY AND HIS MASTERS

9.1   The first sonnet of Sidney's sequence *Astrophil and Stella* is particularly important, because it gives in miniature part of the poetic autobiography and some of the aesthetic ideas of the great poet whom, more than others, I would call 'typically Elizabethan'. Straight away then, read the poem *Loving in truth, and faine in verse my love to show* (Additional Poems 8), making notes on

(i)   Sidney's purpose in writing love poetry

(ii)   his ideas about Invention and Nature in poetry

(iii)   his attitude to other poets

(iv)   any peculiarity in the form of the poem.

9.2   **DISCUSSION**

There is a full discussion of the poem in Alpers (pp. 202–5). If you have access to the book, read that as well as my comments.

(i)   The purpose of writing love poetry is to win Stella's favour; but please observe that this favour ('grace') is expected as an expression of her pity for his suffering, and not because his poetry is expected to arouse her passionate love. Of course, it is a matter of emphasis: the ideas of courtly love and neo-Platonism underlying the first four lines do not exclude the possibility that the reward of physical love will follow the arousal of the lady's mercy and pity. But Sidney's posture is akin to that of religious pleading, and in this he is following neo-Platonic predecessors such as Petrarch, whose response to his Laura was not merely sensuous or possessive, but spiritual. Remember John Ferguson's radio talk on Petrarch in support of Unit 6.

(ii)   Invention is the main thing sought by Sidney, the only quality which will enable him to show his love in verse. It is a quality of Nature ('Nature's child'): that's worth pondering, because it prevents Invention being considered as something artificial in the modern sense, and makes it a harmonious consequence of a sound state of being. We learn from the last line of the poem that Invention is a quality of the *heart*, which was the known seat of the emotions. Yet it is a mistake to imagine that Sidney recommends to himself simple recourse to the emotions as the means of producing good poetry. In the heart of the poet is to be found the eloquence for love which will enable him to transcend mere imitation of other poets.

(iii)   Sidney's attitude to other poets is made perfectly clear from lines 5–8 and 11. He went to the works of other poets in the hope that from them would come fresh inspiration, but reading them, found them not to his purpose. Such a statement seems unexceptionable, until you remember the perspective within which Elizabethan poets saw themselves standing. In their long view of literary history, they were dwarfs in the shadow of the classical poets, especially the Latin poets, of whom Vergil, Horace and Ovid were chief. Between these ancient poets and the Elizabethans stood the Italians of the Renaissance, Ariosto and Tasso, and above all Petrarch. Nearer still, and virtually contemporary, stood the French poets of the Pléiade, among whom

Ronsard and Du Bellay were best known in England. All the poets in these three groups were acknowledged by the Elizabethans as masters: the medieval understanding that masters were to be imitated, with the inference that their essence was to be 'naturalized', was still widely current. During Sidney's lifetime (and he was killed in 1586), nobody in England would have dreamt of claiming, as Vasari did about Italian art at the time of Michelangelo, that native products could actually stand beside those of masters of former times.

(iv)   The peculiarity of form is the length of the line, which contains six iambic feet, instead of the five which is most common in the Elizabethan sonnet and became the rule for English sonnets from that time to the present. In France, the line of six iambic feet had been brought back into use by Ronsard and fellow-poets of the Pléiade, who knew it from the work of Old French poets of the twelfth and thirteenth centuries; and it is from France that Sidney, a great experimenter in metres (see the earlier discussion of *Oh sweet woods, the delight of solitariness*) took the iambic hexameter, or Alexandrine, as it is usually called.

9.3   In the Sidney sonnet which you have just studied, it is that explosive and positively unlofty ' "Foole", said my Muse to me' that marks the kind of individuality, the communing with an urgently-feeling but with-difficulty-disciplined self, which distinguish the best of Elizabethan poetry. And Sidney shows it not only in his sonnets, but in the other forms he uses, when he is at his best. Sir John Davies, listing the poets he wants to emulate at the end of *Orchestra* (stanza 130), describes Sidney the poet in these terms:

> Yet Astrophel might one for all suffice,
> Whose supple Muse chameleon-like doth change
> Into all forms of excellent device.

> Davies, op. cit., p. 47.

To make that description good, read now two of the songs from *Astrophil and Stella*, first, *Who is it that this dark night . . .?* (p. 238 of your anthology), which is the eleventh and last song in the work, and then the eighth song, *In a grove most rich of shade* (Additional Poems 9). Both are in essence dialogue poems, the first continuously so. They are based on conventional situations found in Renaissance courtly love poetry: the first is the wooing at the window, and the second is the lovers' meeting in a grove during May-time, the season of love. Both are poems of defeated love. As you read them, make sure you understand them fully: without making notes, look for the progression or development in each poem, and place within the development any excellences or demerits which you especially notice.

9.4   **DISCUSSION**

9.4.1   I think these are both fine poems, but the more I study them, the more I am aware of differences. The first is organized with strict formality: each stanza begins with two lines spoken by the woman, to which the three lines spoken by the man are a direct reply; and apart from the topping and tailing, in the first two stanzas and the last stanza, each round of the dialogue contains a conventional challenge from a woman who does not intend to accept advances, and a riposte from the man based on neo-Platonic ideas about love. *In a grove most rich of shade* is much more loosely organized: a full setting and a course of action are described, and there is even psychological annotation; and at the centre of the poem, there is not so much a dialogue as a speech and a counter-speech. Both protagonists show marked complexity and individuality of attitude, but it is the woman whose contributions finally make the poem distinguished.

9.4.2   In *Who is it that this dark night* the progression is achieved through the successive refutations by the man of the worldly-wise assumptions of the woman. She says first that his love will change or die, then that he will fall in love with someone else, and then that his reason, or if not that, his suffering, will make him abandon the love-quest. Each refutation by the man contains either an assertion of the permanence and power of his love, or a glittering compliment in the neo-Platonic convention: the first compliment, in stanza 5, makes the lady an Ideal Form of which other women are but 'pictures' or 'images', and the second, in the next stanza, makes his apprehension of her beauty strongest when he employs his reason. The most moving part of the poem, to me, is the man's return from this complimenting to the first assertion of his passion, but this time with a difference: the metaphor of the stake being driven into the 'ground' (which is of course the poet's body) sharply testifies to the man's suffering, and convincingly represents his defiance of the world of fools and louts who oppose his love. The interview ends naturalistically, with the woman's fear that they will be overheard, not psychologically, with a resolution determined by the argument. But, since it is a situation which has been forced on the woman, that is an acceptable and likely ending. A grave and moving poem, the formal structure of which heightens the prevailing mood. (The lute-song setting, by Morley, on the accompanying gramophone record, is particularly fine.)

9.4.3   How different the situation is in *In a grove most rich of shade*. Stella has freely gone to the grove to meet Astrophil, and that act of commitment, however limited it turns out to be, makes possible both action and speech which lie outside the strict confines of the kind of conventional poetry in which the man always begs, and the woman always refuses to grant. Yet the conclusion *is* that conventional one: but the steps by which the conventional position is reached are rich in evidence of a complex relationship between two people of strong emotions and lofty sensibility. The loose structure of the poem allows a free narrative flow in which the varying and sometimes alternating fluxes of passion and circumstance occur without obtrusive artifice: unlike the other, it is a true narrative poem.

> Him great harmes had taught much care,
> Her faire necke a foule yoke bare

gives particularity to a well-known situation, and the ensuing narrative, up to 'Thus to speake in love and wonder' builds up a tremulous atmosphere of love and anguish, out of which the two long speeches break. And between the two speeches, is the realistic action which is symbolic of the whole subject of the poem:

> There his hands in their speech, faine
> Would have made tongue's language plaine;
> But her hands his hands repelling,
> Gave repulse all grace excelling.

Love faced, confessed in full knowledge, and then denied for the sake of honour is the subject, and it is a rare one in poetry. The most striking thing about this particular feminine denial is the consolation offered by Stella. Asked to yield her love because the season invites her to do so, she does not refuse straight away, nor does she question that kind of argument, which is much less lofty than the argument she uses herself. First she acknowledges her love, and only after she has done that strongly and freely does she use the dread word 'deny', and bring in the matter of her honour, which is clearly bound up with the 'foule yoke' – presumably, her marriage with another man. In its conclusion, which is a genuine psychological dénouement, the poem fully expresses the conflicts in a complex and star-crossed love relationship. Besides acknowledging the spiritual domination of the woman, which is orthodox in courtly love and fairly general in Christianized neo-Platonic art and poetry, the poem conveys a sense of ineluctable necessity, by which both woman and man are bound as moral members of society.

9.4.4   A note on the metre of both poems. I hope you felt afresh the haunting quality of the trochees in both poems, and the fastidious manner in which Sidney uses acatalectic or full trochaic lines, such as

> Underneath my window plaineth

in alternation with catalectic lines such as

> It is one who from thy sight.

Sidney varies the trochaic rhythm gently within the line all the time, but the alternation of the feminine endings is deliberate, and provides a firm structure, which is not varied in either poem. If you read the poems aloud, make sure to give syllabic value to the -ed in 'denied', 'placed', 'framed' and so forth when they end the line.

Those three poems give you some idea of the problems Sidney faced, and the way in which he solved them. If Petrarch, his acknowledged master, and often the poet of actual poems which Sidney half-translated and half-adapted, is still too shadowy for you to apprehend, then you should read pages 196–200 of your recommended anthology of criticism, *Elizabethan Poetry*, where David Kalstone, in his essay *Sir Philip Sidney: the Petrarchan Vision*, makes a line-by-line comparison between a sonnet by Petrarch and Sidney's sonnet based upon it.

Petrarch's attitude to love is that, in beholding and describing his lady, he is focusing on a vision of earthly beauty which sustains his spirit in a state of grace analogous with that of the highest religious impulse. She is an attribute of harmonious and beautiful nature, to whom his response cannot be merely sensuous or possessive, but must also be spiritual, as it is to all creations of the mind of God. The difference between his attitude and Sidney's is well demonstrated in the concluding lines of the two sonnets Kalstone discusses. Sidney follows Petrarch in giving the lady all the attributes of perfection, but whereas Petrarch ends by warning that the man who does not hurry to see her while she is young and beautiful will have to weep for ever, Sidney omits the Mutability theme altogether, and ends his contemplation of the lady's beauty with

> 'But ah,' Desire still cries, 'give me some food.'
>
> Ringler, op. cit., p. 201.

With that kind of evidence before him, no contemporary of Sidney's would have suggested that his Stella was imaginary. But a contemporary of Petrarch's did suggest that his Laura was imaginary – a charge Petrarch strongly denied.

10.0 LOVES FORMAL AND INFORMAL

10.1 My purpose in this little section is to provide you with further variety of reading in Elizabethan love poetry before you tackle a group of Shakespeare sonnets. I suggest you read the poems in a swift and concentrated scan, and then my short notes on them: I want you to take on towards the Shakespeare something of their various moods and achievements, so that the more important work to come has a background of the works of other poets in your mind.

10.2 Read the following poems, which I have grouped under the title, 'Loves Formal'.

Let others sing of knights and paladins (p. 79)

How many paltry, foolish, painted things (p. 105)

The nurse-life wheat (p. 138)

Leave me, oh love (p. 240)

10.3 *Notes on 'Loves Formal'*

10.3.1 The first two sonnets, by Daniel and Drayton respectively, are on the theme which Petrarch inherited from Ovid and Horace, almost Christianizing his legacy as he took it over. This is the theme of poetic immortality, which occurs so often in Elizabethan sonneteering as to be worth a developmental study on its own. You might think it an obvious way of proceeding for poets desiring immortality to seek to achieve it by writing of their loved one; but in each poet, and sometimes in each poem, a different emphasis may appear. Consider these separately:

(i) The poet is humble, and thinks his poetry will survive only through the excellence with which his lady's beauty instils it.

(ii) The same, except that the emphasis is on the survival of the lady's beauty in the poetry, and not the survival of the poetry because of the lady's beauty described in it.

(iii) The poet is proud either of his suffering in defeated love or of his own poetic achievement. The beauty of the lady is at one remove, being seen in the context either of the suffering, or of the poetic achievement; but it is not scorned.

(iv) The tables are turned. The lady *may* obtain immortality, of which Mutability would otherwise rob her, only through the excellence of the poetry in which her beauty is described.

Mutability is a factor in all these types, but the more the poet insists on the lady's beauty and its power to survive in verse, the better the consolation and the more hyperbolic the compliment he offers. Of only the first and second types could one say that the theme was 'almost Christianized', because in both the poet tends to immortalize the woman, and abase himself. It is the personal pride in the suffering and in the poetry which provides alternative motivation in the third and fourth types listed above. *Let others sing of knights and paladins* belongs to the first type: the whole poem is an act of worship, and the only counterweight to self-abasement in the parts that relate to the poet is in the subdued triumphal note of

> These are the arks, the trophies I erect,
> That fortify thy name against old age;

The poem ends in modesty and compliment, unlike *How many paltry, foolish, painted things*, in which the poet insists throughout on his power to confer immortality. The worship of the lady is there all right, but the hyperbole is so *studied* –

> Where I to thee Eternity shall give,
> When nothing else remaineth of these days . . .
> So shalt thou fly above the vulgar throng –

that even in context it is hardly credible. Drayton's rejection of all other things except his lady's beauty as 'foolish' or 'vulgar' is rather strained. I find Daniel's emotional involvement with both Delia's beauty and his own poetry more attractive.

10.3.2   The interest of *The nurse-life wheat* lies, for me, in two things: the unity of image (ripeness in nature as a metaphor for the essence of Caelica) and the compression of thought. Spend a moment, if you will, on the relation of the fifth and sixth lines to the ending:

> No less fair is the wheat when golden ear
> Showers unto hope the joys of near enjoying:

and compare the poem and the use of imagery in it, with Peele's *Gently dip, but not too deep*. If you enjoy philosophical poetry, Fulke Greville is for you: he is such a political creature that his ideas of state creep even into his love poetry (see the next poem in the book, *Princes, who have (they say), no mind, but thought*). After a full life, Fulke Greville was murdered by a disgruntled servant who discovered that he was not to benefit under his master's will. Do not be misled, by the way, by the published date of *Caelica*, which is 1633, five years after the poet's death. *Caelica* was 'written in his youth', and Greville was a friend and exact contemporary of Sidney: though the compressed thought of *The Nurse-Life Wheat* has affinities with the 'metaphysical' poetry written somewhat later.

10.3.3   *Leave me, oh love*   There is a difference of opinion about this poem. Lucie-Smith (anthology p. 282) says that it is the true conclusion to *Astrophil and Stella*, but W. A. Ringler Jr., the editor of the latest, and definitive, *The Poems of Sir Philip Sidney*, places it at the end of *Certain Sonnets*, and remarks (p. 434):

> This was only a temporary mood for Sidney, because he continued to work on his *Old Arcadia* and some time afterward composed *Astrophil and Stella*.

The successive images in the poem derive from the stock religious thought *De Contemptu Mundi* (in contempt, or scorn, of this world), and come to a noble climax with the double mention of heaven in the twelfth line. I think it is unimportant whether the poem represents a permanent, or temporary, change in Sidney's thought: the force of conviction is its own explanation and justification. As it is fundamentally a religious poem, you might wonder why I place it amongst love poems. My first reason is that the poem deals with two Loves, the one 'which reaches but to dust' of the first line, which is the point of departure for the poem, and the 'Eternal Love' of the last line. And the second reason is that, since this is the last lofty poem on love in your study course for the time being, I should remind you to what an extent 'Eternal Love' is an essential ingredient in much of Elizabethan love poetry.

10.4   *'Loves Informal'*

This is a title of convenience which I attach to that sort of erotic poetry to which moral and spiritual ideals are scarcely relevant, and in which frankly physical, lustful, cynical or comical aspects of love are the subject. This kind of poetry exists in all ages, and above all in popular poetry (though cynicism tends to appear more in the poetry of aristocratic societies). But towards the end of the sixteenth century it gained a new respectability – artistic respectability, that is, not moral – through the dissemination and admiration of the works of Ovid, whose *Amores* celebrate scandalous love. Look again at Marlowe's translation of the Fifth Elegy from the First Book of *Amores* (p. 182) which you studied in Section 1.9 of Unit 29, to remind yourself exactly of what I mean.

10.5   Profoundly un-Petrarchan, isn't it? But the existence of this kind of poetry in Ovid, whose Latin was a model for the learned world, sanctioned the transfer of its essence to English high poetry, where it enriched the conspectus love poets made of their subject, enabling them to express their 'infected will' as well as their 'erected wit'; and to do this sometimes in terms which justify the transposition of the epithets in those two often-quoted phrases from Sidney. 'Erected will' and 'infected wit' may be essential in the poetic expression of some of the complexities of love; and poets proved it when they began to write poetry which showed that there was no absolute division between the god and the brute in amorous man.

10.6   Now, please read the following three poems, and set the net effect of them in your mind against the effect of the three sonnets you read under the heading 'Loves Formal'. Take more time over *The perfume* because it is the only poem by Donne in your anthology written under the influence of Ovid; and if you like it, you may be encouraged to read more of his work. The reading on the accompanying gramophone record should help you to understand *The perfume*. I offer no following commentary on the poems.

The author to his wife (p. 152)

From Love's Labour's Lost (p. 219)

The perfume (p. 98)

11.0   SIX SHAKESPEARE SONNETS

11.1   The six sonnets chosen for study here all belong to the series written by Shakespeare to a young man, whom I shall call the Friend. They figure in the best sequence of love poems in the English language: I call it a sequence although the way in which they are grouped and ordered is puzzling, and it seems best to assume that they were printed in 1609 without Shakespeare's having revised them or supervised the work, and possibly even in a pirated edition. Before setting you to work on them, I want to indicate some general characteristics of Shakespeare's sonnets which will help you to understand and appreciate the particularity and force of each sonnet you study.

11.2   (i)   The love expressed is a lofty and possessionless one. The poet-lover does not complain of lack of possession except implicitly: his posture is noble, generous and idealistic, and if the Friend is unkind, then the poet treats it as a falling from an ideal standard on the part of the Friend rather than as hostility to himself.

(ii)   The poet's love, though 'lofty and possessionless', and his Friend, are not represented in markedly neo-Platonic terms. Both are of the here and now; the quasi-religious escape of the neo-Platonic position is not open to the poet.

(iii)   The ruling idea – in so far as it is fair to admit to the existence of a *ruling* idea which is more important than the multiform expressions of intense love making up the sonnets – is of Time being defied: defied by the beauty of the Friend, by the love of the poet, and by the expression of these in the poetry which will live to after-times. Eternity is claimed, without religious consolation: the after-life is generally assumed to be posterity, in this living world. Eternity is won by the Friend, through the poetry, not by the poetry, through the Friend.

(iv)   The ruling poetic mode is hyperbole.

(v)   The poems never contain descriptions of the Friend, and seldom assert the circumstances in which any sonnet was written: 'Thy gift, thy tables, are within my brain' (sonnet 122) is a rare exception. But we can infer from some sonnets general circumstances like a quarrel, a falling out of favour, even jealousy of a rival; but the details are not given, and time spent trying to ascertain them is much less well used than time spent working on the poetry.

(vi)   Since the love is possessionless and has no future, since the Friend is idealized, since the poet is free of self-pity, and since heroic defiance of Time is his fundamental posture, I can fairly say that the sonnets embody a tragic view of life.

11.3   There are two good essays in your recommended anthology of criticism, L. C. Knights 'Shakespeare's Sonnets' (Alpers, pp. 274–98) and C. L. Barber: 'An Essay on the Sonnets' (Alpers, pp. 299–320). Read them if you can while studying these six sonnets, preferably after your first reading of the poems, which I shall ask you to read as I direct, and then read my comments:

Shall I compare thee to a summer's day? (p. 231)

Not marble, nor the gilded monuments (p. 232)

Full many a glorious morning have I seen (p. 232)

Farewell! Thou art too dear for my possessing (p. 234)

That time of year thou mayst in me behold (p. 233)

Let me not to the marriage of true minds (p. 235)

11.4   First, two sharply contrasting Eternity sonnets. In what respects are they contrasting, and in what respects similar?

Shall I compare thee to a summer's day?

Not marble, nor the gilded monuments

11.5   **DISCUSSION**

In line 10 of the first of these, 'thou ow'st' = you possess.

Let us take the two octaves first.

In the first sonnet, Shakespeare describes Mutability in summer as a series of racing contrasts, sometimes even within the line, as in 'Rough winds do shake the darling buds of May'. Over all there is glancing light and moving cloud, so that the Friend, who is called 'more lovely and more temperate' than this ravishing seasonal display, catches reflected glory from the beauty of Nature. In the second sonnet, Mutability shows in a Roman mode, as un-cared-for monuments with wars raging amongst them: there is no suggestion that anyone shall compare *them* with the Friend. So Time and Mutability are harder and grimmer here, and in face of them, it will take a more defiant attitude in the sestet to establish the eternity of the Friend.

Then, in place of the mollifying summing-up of

> And every fair from fair sometime declines,

we have the desperately hyperbolic

> Nor Mars his sword nor war's quick fire shall burn
> The living record of your memory.

In the sestets, superficially, the similarities are more marked than the dissimilarities; but let us see to what extent the differences are matters of emphasis and to what extent they are fundamental. In the first sonnet, the marvellous summer of the octave remains within the conspectus for a couple of lines, before personified Death enters with a chill stride: but even he is negative in face of the Friend's beauty – '*Nor* shall death brag . . .'. In the second sonnet, the Friend has to 'pace forth' as a combatant against death, and 'the ending doom' is in prospect rather than the glowing time 'When in eternal lines to time thou grow'st' of the first sonnet. Lastly, the closing couplet of the first sonnet prefigures a kind of eternity co-terminous with mankind, while the closing couplet of the second sonnet takes us to Judgement Day. The light of the one poem, and the dark of the other, are perfectly maintained throughout, though the theme of the two poems is the same.

11.6   Next, read *Full many a glorious morning have I seen*, and trace the meaning as it unfolds through the imagery – because it is manifested nowhere else: there is no plain statement of a meaning for which the imagery might stand metaphorically.

11.7   **DISCUSSION**

Stain = grow dim.

This is one of several sonnets dealing with the Fault of the Friend, or the Estrangement from the Friend. The Friend, who is the 'morning' of the octave and the 'sun' of the sestet, allows himself to be masked by 'the basest clouds' so that he no longer shines on the poet. Perhaps here it is a fault in the Friend, rather than his simple estrangement from the poet: 'basest clouds' seems to imply low company, which the Friend has preferred to Shakespeare. The tender forgiveness and assertion of love in the concluding couplet are the resorts and resources of a really magnanimous spirit, and poetically they are justified by the sheer splendour attributed to the Friend in the first four lines of the poem. That morning, that Friend, brilliantly transfigures whatever he shines on. Note how the shining and the masking of the octave are repeated in the sestet, and how the couplet, which sums up the poet's attitude to his whole subject, is so affirmative in its forgiveness that the fault of the Friend becomes irrelevant. That sun of the world is still shining, though not on Shakespeare.

11.8   Another 'estrangement' sonnet now follows. Again, follow the ruling metaphor through: since its legal and commercial jargon is by no means easy to follow, here are a few notes to help you in the reading of *Farewell! Thou art too dear for my possessing*. They, together with the reading on the accompanying gramophone record, will reinforce your study.

Line

3   'The document which describes your value states that you are free of (unspecified) legal obligations.'

4   (as a result of which) 'My investment in you is ended.'

8   'My title of possession (conferred by the bonds) reverts to you' (Ingram and Redpath, *Shakespeare's Sonnets*, University of London Press, 1964, p. 200).

11   'The great gift' is the love of the Friend for the poet.

12   'Returns to the donor as a result of his second judgement being better than his first.'

11.9   **DISCUSSION**

I know of no poem in which a rare ruling metaphor is so well adapted to successive arguments on a theme. The rather dry technicalities of unpleasantly calculating activities in law and commerce are perfectly attuned to the dreary business of assessing a relationship in a state of breakdown – like the atmosphere in a divorce court. But for the concluding consolation, borne on the poet's magnanimity and his usual blinding sense of the Friend's perfection, that jargon won't do; so for the stroke of pure emotion with which the poem ends, a new metaphor, that of a dreaming king, is used. The final phrase, 'no such matter' is wryly deflationary, coming after the huge pretension of 'In sleep a king'. Shakespeare is nothing if not a realist.

11.10   The next sonnet, *That time of year thou mayst in me behold*, seems to reflect a mood in which the poet has given up trying to defy time. Autumn, twilight, a dying fire, are metaphors for an ageing man. As you read the poem, ask yourself: what unity and development does Shakespeare achieve in managing these images, and what conclusion does he offer?

11.11   **DISCUSSION**

Each of the three metaphors seems obvious enough on the surface, but the order in which they occur, and the extra significance Shakespeare gives to each, intensify the weariness of life's ending, and make more terrifying the coming extinction. Let's see how it works. Autumn leaves are poetic enough, but when you add that the boughs on which they languish 'shake against the cold' and are bereft of birds, and that the boughs are ambiguously called 'choirs', you have felt the chill of death. Then, twilight is sentimentally acceptable as a metaphor for old age, but when you add the 'black night' which succeeds twilight, and turn that night into Death 'that seals up all in rest', you have taken away all hope of continued existence. Now to the fire image, the last one. The horror of this is that the very source of power which 'nourished' life in youth, the combustible material which is now ashes, extinguishes life in old age. As the fire of life gasps for breath, it is suffocated, and the concluding couplet comes as if from the grave-edge. These last words are addressed to the hypothetical witness and not applied to the poet: he is too far gone to benefit from the lesson he is offering. This is one of many poems in which Shakespeare expresses an absolute horror of old age, which he finds loveless, decrepit and ugly.

11.12   In the light of all your work so far, it will be revealing to you, I hope, to return to *Let me not to the marriage of true minds*, my initial discussion of which was limited to the sources of its imagery and its possible didacticism. It would have been wrong to leave it at that. I wrote then (2.12) that the poem demonstrates 'how a poetic convention in the hands of a major poet can seem virtually to disappear under a fusion of original thought and feeling'. Re-read the poem, and listen to the reading of it on the accompanying gramophone record and see whether you agree with me.

11.13   **DISCUSSION**

The trouble with this poem, I believe, is that it is incomparable, so that anything I write about it by way of analysis must fall short of the truth. It is a stupendous assertion of the immortality of true love, which is seen in the central image of the poem as the north star, presiding over storm-tossed humanity and guiding it. Even Time himself is subordinate to that priceless and unshakeable star. Shakespeare is so convinced of love's immortality that for once he doesn't mind old age and the scything down of 'rosy lips and cheeks'. Only 'the edge of doom' reminds us that Love, though the master of Time, is ultimately the servant of Eternity. Assertion upon assertion, with no connecting argument, as there was in, for example, *Farewell! Thou art too dear for my possessing*. And the scheme in which the assertions are made is cosmic, by reason of the star, the huge oceans and storms, Time presiding and Judgement Day looming. The intensely personal style of urgent persuasion ('Let me not . . .' 'Oh no') running through the poem prepares us for the quality of the ending. 'Alteration' has been left, contemptuously, far behind, and when the rhythm is almost complete, the poet is ready with yet another hyperbolic assertion, this time couched in the quiet, simple words of ultimate conviction in the couplet.

12.0   CONCLUSION

12.1   Spenser, Drayton, Jonson, Donne, Sidney, Shakespeare. By way of consolidating your study of Elizabethan poetry, here is one poem of each to work on. All these poems have qualities that you should be able to recognize as a result of your study so far, and I have chosen them because, with the exception of the Spenser sonnet which I place first because it contrasts in this respect, they all express kinds of passion not easily contained within the Petrarchan mould, or the convention of courtly love, or the Christian system of thought which is a partial determinant of both. They all seem to express highly individual passions or perceptions – which is not to say that none of their masters, especially the Latin poets, had not expressed similar passions or perceptions before them.

12.2   I want you to make short notes on the first four poems, describing their characteristics; but to make a close detailed comparison between the Sidney and Shakespeare sonnets, both of which are spoken on the accompanying gramophone record. Both these poems *start* as outbursts against desire; and the differences that then emerge, as well as the kinds of intensity and perception with which they are expressed, will help you to achieve a focus not only on the difference between the two poets, but on two of the best poetic achievements of the age – one characteristic, the other exceptional. The Shakespeare sonnet, by the way, is not one connected with the Friend, but belongs to the group of sonnets (numbers 127–52) associated with the woman who is generally known as the Dark Lady. On the evidence of the poetry, she was a dark vivacious woman with a talent for music, who generally gave him a hard time and in particular was false to him with the Friend.

Let not one spark of filthy lustful fire (p. 251)

An evil spirit (p. 106)

An elegy (p. 165)

The apparition (Additional Poems 10)

Thou blind man's mark (Additional Poems 11)

The expense of spirit in a waste of shame (p. 236)

12.3   **DISCUSSION**

Let not one spark of filthy lustful fire   This is Petrarchan. You should by now be accustomed to the rarefied mood, and the poet's judicious self-abasement. This sonnet perfectly expresses the quasi-religious feeling of neo-Platonic and courtly love. Nothing of Ovid; good old English Puritanism in the first line. Useful to have a reminder of Spenser at this end of your work on poetry.

12.4   *An evil spirit*   Something of the Latin mixture of love and hate (remember John Ferguson's mention of Catullus' 'Odi et amo' (Section 1.3 of Units 5–6), a poem which has inspired countless translations and imitations through the years), together with a common sub-Petrarchan pathos. A bold and thoroughly English closing couplet with a last line exploding in a double paradox.

12.5   *An elegy*   You will have read your editor's note, to the effect that this poem has sometimes been thought to be the work of Donne. Indeed, there is a 'metaphysical' atmosphere about the imagery and the play of ideas through it, and the colloquial and dramatic tone ('Hear, mistress', 'What fate is this?', 'How shall I do?' and so forth) exemplifies that intimacy which appears often in Sidney, and very often in Shakespeare and Donne. These are all qualities Jonson too, often shows. But if I were asked to justify the attribution of the poem to Jonson, I should cite two special qualities:

(i)   The rueful and modest self-deprecation of the four lines from 'Alas, I ha' lost my heat . . .' to ' . . . for my heart'. (You'll find an even more endearing example in *My picture left in Scotland*, which Maurice Hussey, our guest speaker in the radio programme associated with Unit 32, has asked me to include in the correspondence material. Together with his *Why I write not of love*, it's in the additional poems, numbers 7 and 6 respectively.)

(ii)   The combined euphony and gravity, in spite of the lurking humour which renders acceptable the outrageousness of the successive conceits.

The decorum of the poem is classical. The debt to Petrarch is remote, subsisting only in the bare subject matter of a farewell to the beloved. The curt and direct form of address, 'Mistress', rules out any sort of Petrarchan idealism, but does not necessarily reflect adversely on the quality of the poet's love. Listen to the reading on the accompanying gramophone record.

12.6   *The apparition*   Outraged and revengeful scorn, a Latin attitude, may seem more manly than the pathetic, or even than the noble, acceptance of rejection found in courtly love poetry; but only if it is accepted that chivalry and manliness are incompatible. The essence of the Petrarchan position is that the lady can do no wrong, unless her rejection of the lover is called cruel; even then, the 'cruelty' is excused because her behaviour usually manifests her chastity. In this poem Donne goes to the very limits of the unchivalrous, and it is the libellous supernatural fancy, concluding with a savage threat, that leaves me with the feeling that the whole poem is a mere fancy. If it reflects an actual experience, it seems to come from a world of heartless coupling, the world of *Amores*, rather than a world of love. But the vivid horror of the action, which is conveyed by the slow, spell-like sentences, and the sheer wit of the *invention*, which presents us with a scorned lover who in death is all-powerful over the girl who left him, lift the poem above most Elizabethan erotic writing. Consider how much further Donne goes into the real matter of his subject than Drayton with his 'angel–devil'.

12.7   *Thou blind man's mark* and *The expense of spirit in a waste of shame*

12.7.1   Let us look at the form of the poems first. Sidney starts with the formal device of an apostrophe to desire, and punctiliously keeps the very strictest sonnet form. His heavy rhyme scheme is ababbaba bccbcc. Every line is end-stopped. Within the octave and the sestet, the sentence structure follows the divisions and the suggestions of the rhyme scheme, the octave falling into two four-line parts, and the sestet into two three-line parts. The volta is signalled with the decorous 'but', and the three-line conclusion stands separate. A complete Italian sonnet.

12.7.2   Shakespeare turns the familiar English arrangement of the sonnet – three quatrains and a concluding couplet – into a twelve-line cataract of words and phrases all depending on the word 'lust' in the second line, followed by a more or less conventional couplet which comments on the predicament of the lustful. The outpouring is so violent that one is surprised to find the structure of the sonnet, or indeed the structure of any exact poetic form, underneath at all. This is partly because there are major shops in the sense in no fewer than six of the fourteen lines (lines 2, 6, 7, 11, 12, 13). Yet the standard form is there, compressing and dividing the outpouring according to the measure of its parts, and drawing it at its close first to a slower movement, and then to a comparatively reflective synthesis.

12.7.3 Now to the subject matter, beginning with the Sidney. 'Marke' is a target; 'Band' is a swaddling band; 'Web' is cloth in the process of being woven; like Penelope's weaving, its 'end is never wrought'. Blind men and fools are the victims of desire, which is stigmatized as the product of delusive amorous imagination ('Fond fancie') and a string of mental evils. Before going further, compare this opening with Shakespeare's, and you will see at once that, although Shakespeare is still more condemnatory of desire, which he calls lust, he does not even suggest that those who fall prey to it are lacking in any way, either in intelligence or morals. And this is a very significant difference, because it will help determine the respective endings, and affect both our involvement and appreciation.

12.7.4 In the Sidney, the confession of having been a prey to desire begins with the fifth line, and the proposed remedy is clearly stated as early as the eighth. The moral scheme is apparent. The struggle against desire is maintained throughout the first three lines of the sestet – the repeated 'in vaine' making a kind of contest of it – and the conclusion giving the detail of the working out of the cure. The last line but one means 'to seek to express myself only within the bounds of my (true – understood) self'. That excludes desire, which Sidney does not account a part of his 'vertue'. But, lest anyone should imagine that the battle against desire is over once one knows the remedy for it, the final picture is of Sidney hunting all over his psyche in order to get rid of the evil – which must therefore still be there:

Desiring nought but how to kill desire.

The question for the reader is this: has remorse dulled the attractiveness of desire so much that it is no longer a real temptation? The poet's mind was 'mangled' (fine strong word!) by desire: did he at the time believe its wares were worthless, or was this view of them only the result of subsequent remorse?

12.7.5 Turning to the Shakespeare, I cannot help feeling that a different kind of experience lies behind the poem. This is surely no ordinary desire for a woman that is being described, but some particularly compulsive sexual obsession, the indulgence of which strains the very fibres of the being. How else can one account for the first line? Then, be sure you understand *till action*. Until the act of lust is performed, it is 'perjured, murd'rous . . .' and so forth. That is to say, while the lustful man is trying to set up his act of lust he has all those terrible characteristics listed. The rest of the octave takes us on to the mood of self-disgust which succeeds satiety; a mood as madly intense as that which preceded the act of lust. The sestet sums up the horrific antithesis of before and after, and the concluding couplet brings every human being into the experience:

All this *the world* well knows; yet *none* knows well
To shun the heaven that leads men to this hell.

12.7.6 'The Heaven' is the 'joy proposed', the act of lust in anticipation. 'This hell' is the 'very woe' that succeeds; and 'hell' is also, probably, a metaphor for the woman's sexual organ. But the heaven of the poem is delusive, while the hell is real. No remedy is proposed, and so no remedial action can be taken.

To conclude: in the Sidney sonnet, a grave but comparatively unthreatened morality works out its full process in the battle between will and reason, until the point of resolution, both moral and aesthetic (i.e. in relation to the form of the poem) is reached. But the paradox of the last line seems to leave the problem, if not unsolved, at least with further exploration to be done. In the Shakespeare, the reality of the experience of lust remains and dominates the poem, even at the concluding moment of rest, which comes, as it were, when the poet is aghast at, and exhausted by, his experience and his self-recrimination. Will has triumphed, and beaten reason can only comment. The poet neither deludes himself that he is free of his obsession, nor is he free. Hell is still there in the shape of a delusive heaven, as it is for all of us. Such intensity of expression is rarely found, even in the most emotional passages of his plays.

ADDITIONAL POEMS

1   Geoffrey Chaucer: from *The Knight's Tale.*

> . . . Emelye, that fairer was to sene
> Than is the lylie upon his stalke grene,
> And fressher than the May with floures newe –
> For with the rose colour stroof hir hewe,
> I noot which was the fyner of hem two –
> . . . Y clothed was she ffresh, for to devyse;
> Hir yelow heer was broyded in a tresse,
> Bihinde hir bak, a yerde long, I gesse.
> And in the gardin, at the sonne upriste,
> She walketh up and doun, and as hir liste
> She gadereth floures, party white and rede,
> To make a subtil gerland for hir hede,
> And as an aungel hevenysshly she soong.
> . . . This sorweful prisoner, this Palamoun,
> Goth in the chambre, roming to and fro . . .
> . . . And so bifel, by aventure or cas,
> That thurgh a wyndow, thikke of many a barre
> Of yren greet, and square as any sparre,
> He caste his eye upon Emelya,
> And ther-with-al he bleynte, and cride 'A'!
> As though he stongen were unto the herte.

The Knight's Tale 1035–1079

2   Geoffrey Chaucer: from *Troilus and Criseyde.*

> (Troilus) 'O Jove ek, for the love of faire Europe,
> The whiche in forme of bole away thow fette;
> Now help O Mars, thow with thi blody cope,
> For love of Cipris, thou me nought ne lette.'
> O Phebus, thynk whan Dane hirselven shette
> Under the bark, and laurer wax for drede,
> Yet for hire love, O help now at this nede!'
>
> . . . Quod Pandarus, 'Thow wrecched mouses herte,
> Artow agast so that she wol the bite?
> Why, don this furred cloke upon thy sherte,
> And folwe me, for I wol have the wite;
> But bid, and lat me gon biforn a lite.'
> And with that word he gan undon a trappe,
> And Troilus he broughte in by the lappe.

Troilus and Criseyde III 722–42
The Works of Geoffrey Chaucer, ed. F. N. Robinson, Oxford University Press, 1957.

This is the best one volume edition of Chaucer. If you want to read more, I suggest you begin with the Prologue to the *Canterbury Tales*, and then try more of *The Knight's Tale*, the *Miller's and Reeves' (very bawdy) Tales*; the *Pardoner's*, and the *Nun's Priest's Tales*.

3   Christopher Marlowe: *The passionate shepherd to his love*

Come live with me and be my love,
And we will all the pleasures prove,
That hills and valleys, dales and fields,
And all the craggy mountains yields.

There we will sit upon the rocks,
And see the shepherds feed their flocks,
By shallow rivers to whose falls
Melodious birds sing madrigals.

And I will make thee beds of roses
With a thousand fragrant posies,
A cap of flowers, and a kirtle
Embroidered all with leaves of myrtle;

A gown made of the finest wool
Which from our pretty lambs we pull;
Fair lined slippers for the cold,
With buckles of the purest gold;

A belt of straw and ivy buds,
With coral clasps and amber studs.
And if these pleasures may thee move,
Come live with me and be my love.

The shepherds' swains shall dance and sing
For thy delight each May morning.
If these delights thy mind may move,
Then live with me and be my love.

From *The Passionate Pilgrim* (1599)
The Oxford Book of Sixteenth Century Verse, Oxford University Press, 1961.

4   Sir Walter Raleigh: *The nymph's reply to the shepherd*

If all the world and love were young,
and truth in every shepherd's tongue,
These pretty pleasures might me move,
To live with thee and be thy love.

Time drives the flocks from field to fold,
When rivers rage, and rocks grow cold,
And Philomel becometh dumb;
The rest complains of cares to come.

The flowers do fade, and wanton fields
To wayward winter reckoning yields;
A honey tongue, a heart of gall,
Is fancy's spring, but sorrow's fall.

Thy gowns, thy shoes, thy beds of roses,
Thy cap, thy kirtle, and thy posies
Soon break, soon wither, soon forgotten;
In folly ripe, in reason rotten.

Thy belt of straw and ivy buds,
Thy coral clasps and amber studs,
All these in me no means can move
To come to thee and be thy love.

But could youth last and love still breed,
Had joys no date nor age no need,
Then those delights my mind might move,
To live with,thee and be thy love.

From *England's Helicon* (1600), *Oxford Book of Sixteenth Century Verse*, Oxford University Press, 1961.

5   Edmund Spenser: *The Faerie Queene* II.xii.70 ff
Guyon and the Palmer in the Bower of Bliss

70   Eftsoones they heard a most melodious sound,
Of all that mote delight a daintie eare,
Such as attonce might not on living ground,
Save in this Paradise, be heard elsewhere:
Right hard it was, for wight, which did it heare,
To read, what manner musicke that mote bee:
For all that pleasing is to living eare,
Was there consorted in one harmonee,
Birdes, voyces, instruments, windes, waters, all agree.

71   The joyous birdes shrouded in chearefull shade,
Their notes unto the voyce attempred sweet;
Th'Angelicall soft trembling voyces made
To th'instruments divine respondence meet;
The silver sounding instruments did meet
With the base murmure of the waters fall:
The waters fall with difference discreet,
Now soft, now loud, unto the wind did call:
The gentle warbling wind low answered to all.

72   There, whence that Musick seemed heard to bee,
Was the faire Witch her selfe now solacing,
With a new Lover, whom through sorceree
And witchcraft, she from farre did thither bring:
There she had him now layd a slombering,
In secret shade, after long wanton joyes:
Whilst round about them pleasauntly did sing
Many faire Ladies and lascivious boyes,
That ever mixt their song with light licentious toyes.

73   And all that while, right over him she hong,
With her false eyes fast fixed in his sight,
As seeking medicine, whence she was stong,
Or greedily depasturing delight:
And oft inclining downe with kisses light,
For feare of walking him, his lips bedewd,
And through his humid eyes did suck his spright,
Quite molten into lust and pleasure lewd;
Wherewith she sighed soft, as if his case she rewd.

74   The whiles some one did chaunt this lovely lay;
Ah see, who so faire thing doest faine to see,
In springing flowre the image of thy day;
Ah see the Virgin Rose, how sweetly shee
Doth first peepe forth with bashfull modestee,
That fairer seemes, the lesse ye see her may;
Lo see soone after, how more bold and free
Her bared bosome she doth broad display;
Loe see soone after, how she fades, and falles away.

75   So passeth, in the passing of a day,
Of mortall life, the leafe, the bud, the flowre,
Ne more doth flourish after first decay,
That earst was sought to decke both bed and bowre,
Of many a Ladie, and many a Paramowre:

Gather therefore the Rose, whilst yet is prime
For soone comes age, that will her pride deflowre:
Gather the Rose of love, whilst yet is time,
Whilest loving thou mayst loved be with equall crime.

76   He ceast, and then gan all the quire of birdes
Their diverse notes t'attune unto his lay,
As in approvance of his pleasing words.
The constant paire heard all that he did say,
Yet swarved not, but kept their forward way,
Through many covert groves, and thickets close,
In which they creeping did at last display
That wanton Ladie, with her lover lose,
Whose sleepie head she in her lap did soft dispose.

77   Upon a bed of Roses she was layd,
As faint through heat, or dight to pleasant sin,
And was arayd, or rather disarayd,
All in a vele of silke and silver thin,
That hid no whit her alablaster skin,
But rather shewd more white, if more might bee:
More subtile web *Arachne* can not spin,
Nor the fine nets, which oft we woven see
Of scorched deaw, do not in th'aire more lightly flee.

78   Her snowy brest was bare to readie spoyle
Of hungry eyes, which n'ote therewith be fild,
And yet through languour of her late sweet toyle,
Few drops, more cleare then Nectar, forth distild,
That like pure Orient perles adowne it trild,
And her faire eyes sweet smyling in delight,
Moystened their fierie beames, with which she thrild
Fraile harts, yet quenched not; like starry light
Which sparkling on the silent waves, does seeme more bright.

79   The young man sleeping by her, seemed to bee
Some goodle swayne of honorable place,
That certes it great pittie was to see
Him his nobilitie so foule deface;
A sweet regard and amiable grace,
Mixed with manly sternnesse did appeare
Yet sleeping, in his well proportioned face,
And on his tender lips the downy heare
Did now but freshly spring, and silken blossomes beare.

80   His warlike armes, the idle instruments
Of sleeping praise, were hong upon a tree,
And his brave shiled, full of old moniments,
Was fowly ra'st, that none the signes might see;
Ne for them, ne for honour cared hee,
Ne ought, that did to his advancement tend,
But in lewd loves, and wastefull luxuree,
His dayes, his goods, his bodie he did spend:
O horrible enchantment, that him so did blend.

81   The noble Elfe, and carefull Palmer drew
So nigh them, minding nought, but lustfull game,
That suddein forth they on them rusht, and threw
A subtile net, which onely for the same
The skilfull Palmer formally did frame.
So held them under fast, the whiles the rest
Fled all away for feare of fowler shame.
The faire Enchauntresse so unwares opprest,
Tryde all her arts, and all her sleights, thence out to wrest.

82 And eke her lover strove: but all in vaine;
 For that same net so cunningly was wound,
 That neither guile, nor force might it distraine.
 They tooke them both, and both them strongly bound
 In captive bandes, which there they readie found:
 But her in chaines of adamant he tyde;
 For nothing else might keepe her safe and sound;
 But *Verdant* (so he hight) he soone untyde,
 And counsell sage in steed thereof of him applyde.

83 But all those pleasant bowres and Pallace brave,
 Guyon broke downe, with rigour pittilesse;
 Ne ought their goodly workmanship might save
 Them from the tempest of his wrathfulnesse,
 But that their blisse he turn'd to balefulnesse:
 Their groves he feld, their gardins did deface,
 Their arbers spoyle, their Cabinets suppresse,
 Their blanket houses burne, their buildings race,
 And of the fairest late, now made the fowlest place.

84 Then led they her away, and eke that knight
 They with them led, both sorrowfull and sad:
 The way they came, the same retourned they right,
 Till they arrived, where they lately had
 Charm'd those wild-beasts, that raged with furie mad.
 Which now awaking, fierce at them gan fly,
 As in their mistresse reskew, whom they lad;
 But them the Palmer soone did pacify.
 Then *Guyon* askt, what meant those beastes, which there did ly.

85 Said he, These seeming beasts are men indeed,
 Whom this Enchauntresse hath transformed thus,
 Whylome her lovers, which her lusts did feed,
 Now turned into figures hideous,
 According to their mindes like monstruous.
 Sad end (quoth he) of life intemperate,
 And mournefull meed of joyes delicious:
 But Palmer, if it mote thee so aggrate,
 Let them returned be unto their former state.

86 Streight way he with his vertuous staffe them strooke,
 And streight of beasts they comely men became;
 Yet being men they did unmanly looke,
 And stared ghastly, some for inward shame,
 And some for wrath, to see their captive Dame:
 But one above the rest in speciall,
 That had an hog beene late, hight *Grille* by name,
 Repined greatly, and did him miscall,
 That had from hoggish forme him brought to naturall.

87 Said *Guyon*, See the mind of beastly man,
 That hath so soone forgot the excellence
 Of his creation, when he life began,
 That now he chooseth, with vile difference,
 To be a beast, and lacke intelligence.
 To whom the Palmer thus, The donghill kind
 Delights in filth and foule incontinence:
 Let *Grill* be *Grill*, and have his hoggish mind,
 But let us hence depart, whilest wether serves and wind.

     The Poetical Works of Edmund Spenser, ed. J. C. Smith and
     E. de Selincourt, Oxford University Press, 1912.

6   Ben Jonson: *Why I write not of love*

> Some act of *Loue's* bound to reherse,
> I thought to binde him, in my verse:
> Which when he felt, Away (quoth hee)
> Can Poets hope to fetter mee?
> It is enough, they once did get
> MARS, and my *Mother*, in their net:
> I weare not these my wings in vaine.
> With which he fled me: and againe,
> Into my ri'mes could ne're be got
> By any arte. Then wonder not,
> That since, my numbers are so cold,
> When *Loue* is fled, and I grow old.
>
> > *Ben Jonson*, ed. C. H. Herford, P. and E. Simpson, Oxford
> > University Press, 1963, vol. viii, p. 93.

7   Ben Jonson: *My picture left in Scotland*

> I Now thinke, Love is rather deafe, then blind,
> For else it could not be,
> That she,
> Whom I adore so much, should so slight me,
> And cast my love behind:
> I'm sure my language to her, was as sweet,
> And every close did meet
> In sentence, of as subtile feet,
> As hath the youngest Hee,
> That sits in shadow of *Apollo's* tree.
>
> Oh, but my conscious feares,
> That flie my thoughts betweene,
> Tell me that she hath seene
> My hundred of gray haires,
> Told seven and fortie years,
> Read so much wast, as she cannot imbrace
> My mountaine belly, and my rockie face,
> And all these through her eyes, have stopt her eares.
>
> > *Herford and Simpson*, op. cit., vol. viii, p. 149.

8   Sir Philip Sidney: The First Sonnet from *Astrophil and Stella*

> LOVING in truth, and faine in verse my love to show,
> That the deare She might take some pleasure of my paine:
> Pleasure might cause her reade, reading might make her know,
> Knowledge might pitie winne, and pitie grace obtaine,
> I sought fit words to paint the blackest face of woe,
> Studying inventions fine, her wits to entertaine:
> Oft turning others' leaves, to see if thence would flow
> Some fresh and fruitfull showers upon my sunne-burn'd braine.
> But words came halting forth, wanting Invention's stay,
> Invention, Nature's child, fled step-dame Studie's blowes,
> And others' feete still seem'd but strangers in my way.
> Thus great with child to speake, and helplesse in my throwes,
> Biting my trewand pen, beating my selfe for spite,
> 'Foole,' said my Muse to me, 'looke in thy heart and write.'
>
> > *The Poems of Sir Philip Sidney*, ed. W. A. Ringler, Oxford
> > University Press, 1962, p. 165.

9   Sir Philip Sidney: The Eighth Song from *Astrophil and Stella*

> IN a grove most rich of shade,
> Where birds wanton musicke made,
> May then yong his pide weedes showing,
> New perfumed with flowers fresh growing,

Astrophil with *Stella* sweete,
Did for mutuall comfort meete,
Both within themselves oppressed,
But each in the other blessed.

Him great harmes had taught much care,
Her faire necke a foule yoke bare,
But her sight his cares did banish,
In his sight her yoke did vanish.

Wept they had, alas the while,
But now teares themselves did smile,
While their eyes by love directed,
Enterchangeably reflected.

Sigh they did, but now betwixt
Sighs of woes were glad sighs mixt,
With armes crost, yet testifying
Restlesse rest, and living dying.

Their eares hungry of each word,
Which the deere tongue would afford,
But their tongues restrained from walking,
Till their harts had ended talking.

But when their tongues could not speake,
Love it selfe did silence breake;
Love did set his lips asunder,
Thus to speake in love and wonder:

'*Stella* soveraigne of my joy,
Faire triumpher of annoy,
Stella starre of heavenly fier,
Stella loadstar of desier.

'*Stella*, in whose shining eyes,
Are the lights of *Cupid's* skies,
Whose beames, where they once are darted,
Love therewith is streight imparted.

'*Stella*, whose voice when it speakes,
Senses all asunder breakes;
Stella, whose voice when it singeth,
Angels to acquaintance bringeth.

'*Stella*, in whose body is
Writ each character of blisse,
Whose face all, all beauty passeth,
Save thy mind which yet surpasseth.

'Graunt, ô graunt, but speech alas,
Failes me fearing on to passe,
Graunt, ô me, what am I saying?
But no fault there is in praying.

'Graunt, ô deere, on knees I pray,
(Knees on ground he then did stay)
That not I, but since I love you,
Time and place for me may move you.

'Never season was more fit,
Never roome more apt for it;
Smiling ayre allowes my reason,
These birds sing: "Now use the season."

'This small wind which so sweete is,
See how it the leaves doth kisse,
Ech tree in his best attiring,
Sense of love to love inspiring.

'Love makes earth the water drink,
Love to earth makes water sinke;
And if dumbe things be so witty,
Shall a heavenly grace want pitty?'

There his hands in their speech, faine
Would have made tongue's language plaine;
But her hands his hands repelling,
Gave repulse all grace excelling.

Then she spake; her speech was such,
As not eares but hart did tuch:
While such wise she love denied,
As yet love she signified.

'*Astrophil*' sayd she, 'my love
Cease in these effects to prove:
Now be still, yet still beleeve me,
Thy griefe more then death would grieve me.

'If that any thought in me,
Can tast comfort but of thee,
Let me, fed with hellish anguish,
Joylesse, hopelesse, endlesse languish.

'If those eyes you praised, be
Half so deere as you to me,
Let me home returne, starke blinded
Of those eyes, and blinder minded.

'If to secret of my hart,
I do any wish impart,
Where thou art not formost placed,
Be both wish and I defaced.

'If more may be sayd, I say,
All my blisse in thee I lay;
If you love, my love content thee,
For all love, all faith is meant thee.

'Trust me while I thee deny,
In my selfe the smart I try,
Tyran honour doth thus use thee,
Stella's selfe might not refuse thee.

'Therefore, Deere, this no more move,
Least, though I leave not thy love,
Which too deep in me is framed,
I should blush when thou art named.'

Therewithall away she went,
Leaving him so passion rent,
With what she had done and spoken,
That therewith my song is broken.

Ringler, op. cit., p. 217.

10   John Donne: *The apparition*

When by thy scorne, O murdresse I am dead,
And that thou thinkst thee free
From all solicitation from mee,

Then shall my ghost come to thy bed,
And thee, fain'd vestall, in worse armes shall see;
Then thy sicke taper will begin to winke,
And he, whose thou art then, being tyr'd before,
Will, if thou stirre, or pinch to wake him, thinke
    Thou call'st for more,
And in false sleepe will from thee shrinke,
And then poore Aspen wretch, neglected thou
Bath'd in a cold quicksilver sweat wilt lye
    A veryer ghost then I;
What I will say, I will not tell thee now,
Lest that preserve thee'; and since my love is spent,
I'had rather thou shouldst painfully repent,
Then by my threatnings rest still innocent.

The Poems of John Donne, ed. H. J. C. Grierson
Oxford University Press, 1929, p. 43.

11   Sir Philip Sidney: *Thou blind man's marks*

THOU blind man's marke, thou foole's selfe chosen snare,
Fond fancie's scum, and dregs of scattered thought,
Band of all evils, cradle of causelesse care,
Thou web of will, whose end is never wrought;

Desire, desire I have too dearely bought,
With price of mangled mind thy worthlesse ware,
Too long, too long asleepe thou hast me brought,
Who should my mind to higher things prepare.

But yet in vaine thou hast my ruine sought,
In vaine thou madest me to vaine things aspire,
In vaine thou kindlest all thy smokie fire;

For vertue hath this better lesson taught,
Within my selfe to seeke my onelie hire;
Desiring nought but how to kill desire.

Ringler, op. cit., p. 161.

12   Ben Jonson: *Song to Celia* (lute-song on accompanying gramophone record.
Singer: John Elwes. Lutanist: Timothy Davies)

Come my CELIA, let vs proue,
While we may, the sports of loue;
Time will not be ours, for euer:
He, at length, our good will seuer.
Spend not then his guifts in vaine.
Sunnes, that set, may rise againe:
But if once we loose this light,
'Tis, with vs, perpetuall night.
Why should we deferre our ioyes?
Fame, and rumor are but toyes.
Cannot we delude the eyes
Of a few poore household spyes?
Or his easier eares beguile,
So remoued by our wile?
'Tis no sinne, loues fruit to steale,
But the sweet theft to reueale;
To be taken, to be scene,
These haue crimes accounted beene.

Herford and Simpson, op. cit., vol. viii, p. 102.

13   John Donne: *The expiration* (lute-song on accompanying gramophone record)

> So, so, breake off this last lamenting kisse,
> Which sucks two soules, and vapors Both away,
> Turne thou ghost that way, and let mee turne this,
>   And let our selves benight our happiest day,
> We ask'd none leave to love; nor will we owe
>   Any, so cheape a death, as saying, Goe;
>
> Goe; and if that word have not quite kil'd thee,
>   Ease mee with death, by bidding mee goe too.
> Or, if it have, ley my word worke on mee,
>   And a just office on a murderer doe.
> Except it be too late, to kill me so,
>   Being double dead, going, and bidding, goe.
>
>   Grierson, op. cit., p. 61.

14   Shakespeare: *Threnos*

> Beauty, truth and rarity,
> Grace in all simplicity,
> Here enclos'd, in cinders lie.
>
> Death is now the Phoenix' nest,
> And the Turtle's loyal breast
> To eternity doth rest;
>
> Leaving no posterity:
> 'Twas not their infirmity,
> It was married chastity.
>
> Truth may seem, but cannot be;
> Beauty brag, but 'tis not she;
> Truth and beauty buried be.
>
> To this urn let those repair
> That are either true or fair:
> For these dead birds sigh a prayer.
>
>   *The Poems*, ed. F. T. Prince, Methuen, 1961.

SOME SUGGESTIONS FOR FURTHER READING

Apart from generally encouraging you to read more Elizabethan and Jacobean poetry, I want to suggest that, if you are serious about developing a deeper experience of the poetry of the age, the best thing you can do is to explore defined areas in a concentrated way. To this end I offer three tasks, each based on a limited amount of poetry supported by specific critical texts. I place the Shakespeare task first because I think it's the one most likely to give you the greatest benefit. But it is up to you whether you then go on to Spenser or Donne. If studying this whole course has awakened in you a deep feeling for the Renaissance, then probably you should further explore the mind and art of Spenser. But if your interest lies in the end of the period, and the development of a way of thought and expression more akin to the modern then it is to Donne that you may wish to turn.

1   Shakespeare's Sonnets

Suggested text: *Shakespeare's Sonnets* ed. W. G. Ingram and T. Redpath, University of London Press, 1964. This is a very fully edited text, in which explanation and annotation of the poems often become discussion. But the full annotation cannot take the place of good criticism.

Suggested critical support text: *Themes and Variations in Shakespeare's Sonnets* by J. B. Leishman, Hutchinson, 1961.

Another useful book, which deals with other sonneteers of the period besides Shakespeare, is *The Elizabethan Love Sonnet* by J. W. Lever, Methuen, 1956.

2   Spenser's 'The Faerie Queene'

Suggested text: The Oxford *The Poetical Works of Edmund Spenser*, ed. J. C. Smith and E. de Selincourt, 1912 and frequently re-printed, is a standard text and has a useful glossary, but the print of the one-volume edition is small and in double columns. To read the whole of *The Faerie Queene* with critical understanding is an experience many students, even students of Honours English, strangely deny themselves.

Suggested critical support texts: There is a good deal of useful Spenser criticism in your recommended text for Units 29–30: *Elizabethan Poetry: Modern Essays in Criticism*, ed. J. Paul Alpers, Oxford University Press, 1967. A good book to keep by you while reading the poem is *A Preface to The Faerie Queene* by Graham Hough, Duckworth, 1962. Parts One and Two provide a sound introduction, and Part Three consists of a book-by-book commentary on the poem.

3   John Donne's Songs and Sonets

Suggested text: *The Song and Sonets of John Donne*, ed. T. Redpath, Methuen, 1956. Again, this volume contains very full annotation and explanation of the poems. In addition, there is a useful general introduction to the poetry of Donne.

Critical support texts: A good introduction to Donne's life and work is the introductory essay by H. J. C. Grierson, in his edition of *The Poems of John Donne*, Oxford University Press, 1929. The single book on Donne that I find most useful, and therefore recommend, is *The Monarch of Wit*, by J. B. Leishman, Hutchinson, 1951.

ACKNOWLEDGEMENTS

Grateful acknowledgement is made to the following for material used in these units:

The Athlone Press of the University of London for Agnes Latham, *Sir Walter Raleigh Selected Prose and Poetry*; Chatto & Windus Ltd. for Rosemary Freeman, *English Emblem Books*; Penguin Books Ltd. for E. M. W. Tillyard, *The Elizabethan World Picture*.

Notes

Notes

RENAISSANCE AND REFORMATION